KEN ROSSIGNOL

CHESAPEAKE 1880

CHESAPEAKE 1880

The lives of the Ethan Aaron Douglas family in the
Tidewater Region of Chesapeake Bay

KEN ROSSIGNOL

CHESAPEAKE 1880

KEN ROSSIGNOL

CHESAPEAKE 1880

Dedicated To Kaitlyn

ISBN-13: 978-1505334432

ISBN-10: 1505334438

Second in the Series

Robert W. Walker, Editor
Robert W. Walker books
Cover by Elizabeth Mackey

Credits:
Thanks to the Library of Congress and the
wonderful historians and librarians who have worked so
diligently to preserve American heritage.
The author's great appreciation is extended to the
many who have donated various books, articles, prints,
photos and other documents; and to the taxpayers who
have made it all possible to preserve this important
history. The Library of Congress has been a blessing in
being able to produce this book and readers
everywhere are encouraged to use its resources.

Most of the histories of the Chesapeake region presented in this volume is painstakingly accurate with some embellishment and fictional scenarios connected with the story line of the fictional characters. Otherwise, authentic historical recitations with real figures presented here are accurate to the best ability of the author and reliance on historical news accounts of the era.

Considerable appreciation to the following: The Baltimore American, The Baltimore Sun, The Bee, The Washington Herald, The Weekly Register, The Norfolk Virginian, The Enoch Pratt Free Library, the Maryland Historical Society, The Johns Hopkins Press, Fire Museum of Maryland, National Board of Fire Underwriters, Chesapeake Bay Maritime Museum, Deltaville Maritime Museum, Calvert Marine Museum, Talbot County Historical Society, The St. Mary's Beacon, St. Mary's County Historical Society, The Washington Evening Star, The Washington Post, The Washington Times, The Chesapeake Today, Bain News Service, Detroit Publishing, New York Public Library, Baltimore & Ohio Railroad, C & O Railroad, Maryland Archives, Pepper Langley, Larry Millison, Larry Jarboe, Patrick Buehler, Joyce Bennett, John P. Rue, J. Richard Knott, Fred & Beth McCoy.

Oyster Wars

On December 10, 1888, the oyster police steamer *Gov. Robert M. McLane* battled oystermen who were illegally dredging on the waters of Chester River. After the 4-hour battle, Thomas Howard, commander of the McLane prevailed. Two of the dredge boats, the pungies *JULIA JONES* and *J.C. MAHONEY*, were sunk, and a third boat was captured.

The organizer of the dredgers, Captain Gus Rice of the *J.C. MAHONEY* was jailed in Queenstown. It was the last incident of the "Oyster Wars" in which the dredgers put up such determined resistance to law enforcement.

KEN ROSSIGNOL
Contents

Foreword

The *Express*

The following reports were published in the St. Mary's Beacon, Leonardtown, Md., describing the wreck of the *Express:*

St Mary's Beacon, 10/31/1878
Loss of the Express

We remember no event as occurring within our newspaper experiences which has cast deeper and wider gloom in our community than that which has occasioned by the loss of the steamer *Express* in the terrible storm on the Chesapeake on Wednesday morning of last week. The Steamer left her wharf in Baltimore at the usual hour on Tuesday evening, though storm signals are reported to have been flying from all prominent points in the city. In all the sad details, we find nothing to fault Capt. Barker, except in his disregard of this warning, and at present writing, we don't know that the criminal cupidity of the boat's owners is not more responsible for this than the Captain. However, this may be the steamer proceeded down the bay without encountering any serious difficulty until about midnight. She was then off Patuxent River and soon after struck a high east wind, which by four, o'clock Wednesday had changed to a Southeast and increased to a hurricane. At this point of time, Barker locates the position of the Steamer as between Point No Point and Barren Island. Finding that the strain on the vessel would be fatal that it would be impossible to weather the gale or make the Potomac, he headed for the eastern Shore, which was the nearest at hand. The sea, the Captain states, boarded the steamer by the forward gang plank and ran clear aft to the wheel house, badly straining the joiners work and filling the fire and coal rooms. The immense amount of water shipped caused the vessel to tile to the starboard. Finding her getting lower and lower as she careened, the freight was thrown over and an attempt was made to get her up by letting go the anchors. Even this proved unavailing. At 5:30 o'clock the hurricane deck was wrenched away and the saloon went to pieces. Mr. Francis J. Stone, purser of the lost steamer supplies the following thrilling particulars of the final catastrophe:

"Every man in the crew stood at his post to the last and not one instance of flinching or panic was seen. The officers and men stayed below, throwing cargo overboard to lighten the steamer; were assisted by several passengers until the furnace fires were out and it was known to be useless to try to save the boat. The lady passengers were calm and resigned. Not one cry of terror was heard. The ladies assisted each other to put on life preservers. These preparations were silently made for that fight for life, which all saw was inevitable. An audibly utter prayer here and there, a moan of suppressed emotion from one or another of the passengers in the saloon were all the outward evidences given the intense feeling which possessed the breasts of all on board. In the meantime, the *Express* was falling over as each wave struck her, and she could not recover from the successive shock. The people helped each other up the now perpendicular side, where the steamer rested, but a brief period and the next wave tumbled her completely over. The upper work parted from the hull, and all who were not immediately drowned were floated off on whatever pieces of the wreck they could grasp. Mr. Ullman, two colored female passengers, and Mrs. Tarleton and child did not so far as Mr. Stone knows, get clear of the boat. He thinks they went under when the vessel turned bottom upward. When those who were swept off cleared the hull about two minutes were allowed for everyone to do all the good, he could. Mr. Stone had on his underclothes only having stripped for the struggle, except that he was caught with his overcoat, the climax having come so quickly that he had not time to throw it aside. One of the officers helped him to get rid of the coat in the water, and his limbs were freed. An attempt was made to get Mrs. Bacon and Mrs. Jones into a yawl, but no boat could live in such a sea, and both ladies were drowned. While, for a short time, the people in the water were to the leeward of the wreck they were sheltered from the gale and could keep themselves and each other in selecting a piece of timber, planks, etc. The darkness and the emergency required prompt action. When the rafts drifted clear of the hull and were struck by the waves helping one another was out of the question. Dr. Burch held on to the rail as long as he could, and three times was saved by others when his hold was breaking, but at last he was swept away and lost. Mr. Stone could at first trace out each group on every raft. Hawkins, a fireman on the *Express* had stood at his post on the steamer until waist deep in water. On the raft, he was equally cool and courageous. Willie Barker, the lad on another raft was at first demoralized, and one of the men held on to him manfully, besides taking care of himself. When the boats from the Shirley came to the rescue all hands on the raft were benumbed and well-nigh exhausted. Mr. Stone does not believe that any of the female passengers of the Express was saved. Mrs. Isaacs' chambermaid was seen on a mattress, and she had a life preserver on, but was swamped in the debris around her. The two colored women passengers were never seen after the saloon parted from the hull and broke in pieces. The three ladies were almost instantly drowned within a few minutes of the disaster. Mr. Stone thinks that the two Carrington's were carried into Hungary River and that they and perhaps others may be saved.

There were on board the ill-starred boat at the time of the disaster besides the officers and crew which consisted of 21 persons and eleven passengers making thirty-two in all, and of the whole number, about sixteen are believed to have been saved. We give below the names of such of the lost as are of special interest to our readers: - Mrs. M. A. Jones, wife of Capt. Randolph Jones; Mrs. M A. Bacon, relict of the late Dr. Bacon; Mrs. Pinkney Tarleton and son, aged 6 years; Dr. D.C. Burch; Leonard J. Howard, first officer of the Steamer; Henry Ullman, well known here as a cattle buyer. It is believed there were some colored people belonging to the county also lost, but we have as yet been unable to ascertain their names. Four of the bodies of the drowned have been recovered. Two are those of ladies, probably Mrs. Bacon and Mrs. Jones from the description given of them and the others are bodies of men, both white. A body believed to be that of Mrs. Jones is buried on Adam's Island and the other three on Long Island. All of these had life preservers attached.

St Mary's Beacon, 11/7/1878
Bodies Recovered

We learnt through private sources that the bodies of Mrs. Randolph Jones, Mrs. Dr. Bacon, and Mrs.

Pinkney Tarleton have been recovered by friends and relatives and given sepulture. The first in Philadelphia, and the two last named in our county. The body of Mr. L. J. Howard, first officer of the Express, has also been obtained and interred in Baltimore. At latest accounts, neither the bodies of Dr. Burch, Mr. Ullman nor the child of Mrs. Tarleton had been found.

St Mary's Beacon, 11/7/1878

Who is Responsible? (From the Washington Gazette)

The *Express* and other steamers. Violent storms, such as the one that swept along our coast ten days since; and old decayed steamboats never did get along well together. Sailors will tell you that in nine cases out of ten the old steamboat gets the worst of it and that it was due to a merciful Providence that she did not go to the bottom with all on board. Some time ago we referred in these columns to the fact that the placid waters of the Potomac were regarded by ship-owners north of us as a good enough graveyard for their old, worn-out steamboats – craft of a kind they could find no employment for elsewhere and what is more these persons mean mercenary and reckless of human life find respectable persons here read to land themselves in keeping afloat, at the risk of human life, these old and dangerous boats.

It is not our intention to censure anyone for the terrible loss of life on the Express and other old and unsafe steamers; but to point out where in our opinion, the evil lies and to invite the Government to apply proper remedies. We say because every careful observer of such terrible disasters as the one to which we just referred must admit that there is gross trifling with human life somewhere and that it rests with the

Government to find out the parties responsible for it and administer such punishment as shall be a warning for the future.

In England, the natural lifetime as it is called, of a wooden hull steamship is eight, ten and twelve years according to the condition and character of the wood as well as the workmanship and fastening. Here men prolong the natural life of a steamboat to an almost indefinite period. We do not know what scientific reasoning this is done; but it is done and done until a violent storm puts an end to the old craft's life by sending her to the bottom with all on board save perhaps one or two to tell the terrible tale of suffering and death. Can it be that there is something radically wrong about our system of "Government Inspection?" The number of cases recently brought to our notice where Government inspectors had given certificates directly opposite to the facts as well in regard to hulls as boilers leads us to the belief that many of the inspectors are either grossly incompetent or criminally corrupt. We have heard old navy officers charge them with both.

The circumstances attending the wreck of the *Express* will forcibly illustrate the truth of what we have been staying. That steamer was built in New York about thirty-eight or thirty-nine years ago; if we remember right to run in connection with the Long Island Railroad. She was not suited for the purpose, and we believe another boat was built to take her place. She sat very low in the water, had an old fashioned square engine with high counter balance – a type of engine obsolete more than twenty years ago. She was not fast and has been represented recently, and we are informed that it was with the greatest difficulty twenty pounds of steam would be kept on her. In truth, she has not power enough to stem an ordinary gale or as the sailors say look an ordinary sea in the face, and the wonder is that she had not gone to the bottom long ago. But let us go back to this boat's history.

We lost sight of the *Express* in the waters of New York for several years. On the outbreak of war, low and behold our old acquaintance turned up in the waters of the Chesapeake, ready to do duty in connection with the Army of the Potomac. There were quite a number of old, worthless steamboats which had been laid up along the banks of the Hudson for a number of years. These of a sudden were tinkered up brought around into the Potomac and made to do their duty in transporting troops in the end proving a mine of wealth to their patriotic owners. Conspicuous among these worthless vessels were the *Hero,* the *Catskill,* the *Croton* and the *Hudson*. Mr. Secretary Cameron (Simon) appointed one of his favorites, a Mr. Tucker who had held some position in a New York hotel, to the position of chartering vessels for transportation of troops and as was afterwards shown, Mr. Tucker thought anything was good enough to carry soldiers. The *Express* was perhaps, the best of this class of boats, but even then she was called old, and her sea-going qualities doubted. We are told, however that she had very recently been rebuilt at the expense of sixteen or eighteen thousand dollars. Those acquainted with ship building and ship repair knew very well what that means. It means little more than putting new topsides on an old bottom, etc. and we have always doubted whether it added strength to the hull as a whole. The Government steamer *Tallapoosa* under the manipulation of that pair of patriots Robert and John Andrew Jackson Creswell underwent the same sort of rebuilding at a cost to the Government of $247,000.

That the *Express* was not seaworthy is shown by the fact the *Lady of the Lake* was out in the same gale and weathered it, not because of any skill in handling her, but because she was staunch and seaworthy. We hope the Government will make a thorough investigation of this matter that the public may know who is responsible for this sad loss of human life.

St Mary's Beacon, 11/14/1878

Other Bodies Recovered

A correspondent of the *Sun*, under date of the 19th of November, instant, writes that the Captain of an oyster pungy from Crisfield picked up the body of a lady afloat near the eastern shore of the bay, and finding upon it a "scapula and other articles which are generally worn by Catholics," proceeded to Potomac and landed it at a home in St. Inigoes neck which he knew was the property of them to say it proved to be the identical house in which Mrs. Tarleton was born and the body was identified as hers. The body of her child has also been found on the bay shore near "Point No Point". They are the last of the missing victims of the Express disaster except Dr. Burch.

St Mary's Beacon, 11/14/1878 (page 2, column 4)

Express Officer Asserts Captain Acted Properly

To the Editors –

I feel it incumbent upon me as an officer of the late Steamer *Express* and the only one residing in this community, to make a plain statement of facts in connection with her loss, hoping that time having cooled the general excitement, the public mind may now be in condition to form a calmer and just judgment. With this object in view, I respectfully solicit the use of your columns for that purpose.

Since my return home, I have heard with deep regret and reproach unjustly came upon the conduct of the owners, officers and those concerned in the management of the vessel.

The *Express* sailed a little after 4 o'clock on her regular day, being detained a few minutes in taking on freight, which arrived late, and without the slightest interference on the part of the owners or others to detain her. The weather had been fair during the evening but was beginning to cloud a little, with the wind from the eastward, but with no signs of approaching storm, and not a storm signal was shown. Knowing as I did the vessel to be staunch and strong, I neither saw nor apprehended danger. The weather continued cloudy and about 10 o'clock it commenced to rain, at least I was awakened about that time, and heard it raining, but with very little increase of the wind. It was not until 12.30 o'clock that I was aroused by the heavy roll of the sea and got up to find the storm upon us.

The storm or cyclone burst upon us with such fury and violence that man's efforts were futile to arrest the consequence and the result that followed. For five mortal hours, the *Express* withstood the wringing and wrenching of the raging storm and justified to the fullest my opinion of her seaworthiness. None but an eye-witness could comprehend and appreciate the terrific and terrible force of this to me unprecedented hurricane. With those facts known to me, and all on board the vessel, no censure or reproach can rightly be sustained or even intimated, without being more a reflection and reproach upon God's mysterious and wonderful workings than any shortcomings or lack of forethought and judgment on the part of man.

An investigation of all the circumstances attending the disaster was held at the custom house in Baltimore by the proper authorities, and after all the evidence had adduced, the Inspectors expressed themselves satisfied that Capt. Barker and his crew had done everything in their power to avert the calamity.

 Nov. 14, 1878
 F.J. Stone

INTRODUCTION:

The Old Bay Line President Ethan Aaron Douglas ordered that ten copies of the following publication be made available on each sailing of the steamships of the Company and replenished as often as needed. The passengers were invited to take a copy of *The Chesapeake Illustrated* with them as they disembarked. Herein to introduce CHESAPEAKE 1880 is the 1879 publication *The Chesapeake Illustrated* in its entirety.

Having seated ourselves, comfortably, on one of the magnificent steamers that daily leave dear old Baltimore to traverse the waters of our noble Chesapeake, we are prepared to inhale the exhilarating breeze, and with interest view the numerous attractions along her historic banks.

As we float swiftly, but noiselessly along, probably the eye of the traveler will first be attracted by a beautiful and lofty bank on the right side of the river known, familiarly, as Federal Hill. Memory recalls the glorious happy event that not only illustrated American ingenuity, but gave an immortal name to one of Baltimore's most prominent landmarks. In July, 1788, in honor of the ratification of the Constitutions, a grand procession of merchants, seamen, tradesmen and others was formed, a prominent feature of which was a small but fully rigged shipped, called the "Federalist" mounted on wheels and drawn by horses. After the float being paraded through the principal streets, the boat was finally "anchored" on this spot. And thus it was from this ingenious contrivance of Capt. Barney that a name was given to one of the most illustrious places of historic interest. During the late civil war, Federal Hill was occupied by General B. F. Butler. Massive bulwarks were thrown around the crown of the hill, and about fifty guns were ever ready for immediate action.

CRAIGHILL'S CHANNEL RANGE OR LEADING LIGHTS,
CHESAPEAKE BAY.—THE HIGH LIGHT.

Baltimore Sun building circa 1900.

Next claiming our notice is the Boston Steamship Pier, on the left bank of the river, foot of Long Dock. From this pier, magnificent steamships are continually leaving for Boston (via Norfolk), Providence and Savannah. Our attention is now attracted by the immense building formerly known as Calvert Sugar Refinery.

In a short time the traveler will observe on the opposite bank of the river, the works of the Maryland Fertilizing Company, and soon he is abreast of what is well known to all Baltimorean as Locust Point. This prominent location is indeed valuable land, situated on the south bank of the Patapsco at the northern extremity of Whetstone Point; it was formerly solely on account of its coal trade. But passing time has wrought a change, for magnificent ocean steamers find here convenient piers in what was once dirty, coal-begrimed and otherwise unsightly wharves. The docks being 100 feet wide are capable of accommodating several vessels at once. To encourage the grain trade, the enterprising Baltimore and Ohio Railroad Company have built two immense grain elevators; the capacity of which is over 2,000,000 bushels of grain. There is construction on the same side of the river one of the largest dry docks in the United States. Almost immediately opposite, at the extremity of Fells Point, are numerous wharves, docks and warehouses belonging to the Northern Central Railroad. This energetic company, ever ready to improve its shipping facilities and advance the interest of Baltimore, have built three immense grain elevators. The most conspicuous of these is situated in deep water, and 660 feet long and is capable of holding 600,000 bushels of grain.

And now we're within sight of the most prominent and historically interesting place that meets the eye of the excursionist – Fort McHenry. This important post was named in honor of Col. James McHenry. During the Revolutionary War, it was quite formidable. The fort provided considerable service to the young nation. The grandest epoch in her history is the 12th and 13th of

September, 1814, the time of the terrible bombardment by the British. Doubtless the history of her glorious resistance is familiar to all our readers; surely all true, patriotic Americans are aware that during this frightful engagement, Francis Scott Key wrote the "Star Spangled Banner."

Fort McHenry cannons at the ready.

Opposite Fort McHenry is the Lazaretto Light House. From this point to the extremity of Whetstone Point, an imaginary line may be drawn defining the city limits. We are now fairly on the Patapsco; the branches having met; the river perceptibly widens.

Looking to our left, about two miles inland, and a little back of us, we have a fine view of the Baltimore City Almshouse, otherwise Bayview Asylum. This building was erected at a cost of over a half-million dollars and is surrounded by forty-six acres of rich, cultivated land.

On the same side but near the river bank is a popular resort known as Riverside View, and boasts a long brown, peculiarly built, elevator.

Opposite and near the northern extremity of dear old Anne Arundel County is the Marine Hospital. Foreign vessels seeking to enter the port of Baltimore are compelled to stop within what is called the "line of quarantine." Medical authorities examine the vessel, and if all on board are found free from contagious diseases, the boat is allowed to enter the city harbor. If not, the sick are consigned to the Marine Hospital; the vessel fumigated, and sometimes when it is necessary; her whole cargo unloaded before she is allowed to leave Quarantine Station.

Steamboats in port in Baltimore. Library of Congress

A short distance further, on the Anne Arundel side, we note the mouth of Curtis Creek and at a distance of one mile, Hawkins Point Lighthouse. This location is about seven miles from Baltimore, and the lighthouse built in six feet of water with white fixed lights.

Bear Creek indents the shore of Baltimore County almost immediately opposite.

CHESAPEAKE 1880

Nearly in the middle of the river is a large but useless fort, dignified by the name of Fort Carroll, but never called into action, it sank into insignificance.

This structure, although never completed, was commenced a few years prior to the late war, and designed as a defense to the harbor of Baltimore. In an architectural point of view, it was just what was wanted; presenting as it does eight perforated granite sides of fronts, and would seem an impossible barrier to any invading foe.

The flag that flew over Fort McHenry during bombardment.

But the experience in the late war and the improvements in the art of gunnery have satisfied the Government that it could not resist a formidable attack. The structure was, therefore, never completed.

Grand in its conception and a masterpiece of engineering, it was constructed by the late General Robert E. Lee, of the Confederate Army, who was then an officer in the U. S. Service.

Fort Carroll is now used as a Government Lighthouse.

Near the Anne Arundel shore, some immense rocks project from the water.

Inland from these there was formerly a celebrated summer resort called, very appropriately, White Rock Retreat.

On the Baltimore County side, directly opposite, is an arm of the river called Old Road Bay, bordering on which there is a magnificent grove of trees. Need we mention that this is a beautiful and popular resort, and was once called Holly Grove and that it has now received the most suitable name of North Point Tivoli? For several years crowds of thoughtless pleasure seekers have sought the sylvan shades and romantic scenery of Holly Grove, all unconscious that they were near the hallowed ground of North Point. Now the woods and glens of resound to laughter and merriment where little less than a century ago, General Ross, flushed with his success in the National Capital, disembarked with his 9,000 men, hoping to make a

successful entrance into

President's House, after its destruction by the British

The White House after being burned and sacked by the British in 1814.

Baltimore and march triumphantly through Maryland. But he was met by a band of heroes, as superior in bravery as they were inferior in number, determined to die, if need be, in defense of their firesides; but to lose their lives dearly. The whole number of Americans did not exceed 3200 men, and of these but 1700 were engaged when General Ross was killed and his successor, General Brooks, withdrew his army. A small remnant of the "Old Defenders," in our city, still celebrate the anniversary of their glorious repulse of the invading force; but the Great Reaper has spared but few, and as they now gather together on the 12th of September, the silvery locks, attenuated frames and palsied limbs bear but slight resemblance to the gallant soldiers of 1814. Death will soon call the last of the noble band hence, but their memory will be a sacred legacy to their country.

The attractions of North Point Tivoli are indeed numerous. A large and handsome pavilion; a first-class Restaurant; beautiful shady with walks afford true pleasure for the "merry lads and lassies" that daily throng this pleasant summer resort. Swings, flying horses, and other sources of amusement delight the little ones. It seems to be the earnest endeavor of the Proprietor, Mr. Frank Debelius, to please his patrons in every possible manner.

Two magnificent government lighthouses have recently been erected at the extremity of North Point proper.

And now we are upon the glorious old CHESAPEAKE. As the traveler scans the surrounding surface of the bay, a lighthouse, called the Seven Foot Knoll, appears at no great distance. How lonely, how deserted, but yet how wakeful must be the keeper of that solitary light! Let us fancy ourselves in this lone, seemingly-forsaken place during the long and dreary nights of winter. Surrounded by an almost impassable barrier, and miles from civilization, trembling with fear lest the huge blocks of ice that gather about and driven by the wind shake the dwelling, should demolish the weak and fragile frame that supports us!

CHESAPEAKE 1880

After passing old Bodkin Point, four miles of cultivated land and Gibson Island, we have on the Anne Arundel side, Stony and Persimmon Points guarding the mouth of the Magothy River. While immediately opposite we have entrance to the Chester River, the southern boundary of Kent County.

Since numerous excursionists and other travelers are continually leaving Baltimore on a trip to the charming village of Chestertown, and not knowing but what our reader may be one of these, we will take a cursory view of the town, apologizing to the patient reader should he be bound for a more distant resort. A ride of about 25 miles up the beautiful Chester River brings us to the county seat of Kent. Chestertown is 60 miles from Baltimore and has a population of 2,000. The inhabitants are noted as a generous, hospitable and industrious people. The venerable Washington College, (organized 1783), is within ten minutes' walk of the steamboat landing. This college is an institution of great merit. Near the college is a beautiful burial place called Chester Cemetery. Large warehouses and magnificent dwellings told us that rich merchants and retired me appreciate the advantageous and picturesque situation of Chestertown.

Going "UP THE BAY"

Tolchester Beach, the nearest and probably the most popular of all the "Up the Bay" or more properly speaking, "Across the Bay" resorts, is situated on the Eastern Shore, and nearly opposite the mouth of the

Patapsco. It is about 25 miles from Baltimore, and through the summer is reached twice daily by the Steamer *Pilot Boy*.

—TO—

TOLCHESTER BEACH

PARK AND LAKE.

THE STEAMER

"PILOT BOY."

Leaves Baltimore from Pier 9½ Light Street.

TWICE DAILY.

AT 8.15 A. M., AND 2.30 P. M.

RETURNING—LEAVES THE BEACH AT 10.15 A.M., and 6.30 P. M.

ARRIVING IN BALTIMORE ABOUT 12 and 8.15 P. M.

ROUND TRIP TICKETS.

ADULTS..50 CENTS.
CHILDREN 6 to 12 years ....25 CENTS.
CHILDREN UNDER 6 ....NO CHARGE.

☞*Special Rates for Parties of 25 or Over.*

☞VERY LOW RATES TO CHURCHES, SCHOOLS AND SOCIETIES.

For further particulars, apply to

W. C. ELIASON, on the Steamer Pilot Boy,

BALTIMORE, June 1st, 1890.   PIER 9½ LIGHT STREET.

The principal attraction at Tolchester is the excellent bathing beach. The western winds which prevail in the summer blowing over an expanse of 20 miles of salt water, and excellent perch fishing are Nature's contributions to Tolchester. A large new dining room and restaurant with piazzas 130 feet long, commanding a fine view of the bay, has been erected. Several large pavilions prettily located in the woods and on the bluff, rustic bridges, shooting galleries and ten-pin alleys, and above all, gentlemanly and self-respecting people in charge of all departments combine to render this trip one of the most delightful leaving Baltimore. Special conveniences are arranged for ladies and children while the attractions for the younger generation are all amply provided by the proprietor, Mr. W. C. Eliason. The management is to be congratulated on the select excursion parties that daily visit their attractive retreat.

After passing Tolchester Beach, the next feature of interest will be on our left and is a small island name of Pool's Island. This desirable place for a summer resort is two miles from Harford County shore and four miles from the shore of Kent County. It contains 280 acres, 200 of which are in a high state of cultivation. Some six years ago, 7,000 peach trees were planted which now are in full bearing. Fishing, crabbing, gaming, and sea-bathing are among its attractions. After passing the island on our cruise, the bay becomes gradually narrower until we are off of Howell's Point and nearly at the mouth of the Sassafras River. At this point, the river is only about three miles in width. As we near the beautiful and commercial Elk River, (4 miles distant) the Chesapeake suddenly widens.

The Ericsson Line of Steamers, plying between Baltimore and Philadelphia, pass up along the Elk River, thence into Back Creek and enter the locks of the Chesapeake and Delaware Canal at Chesapeake City. This town is advantageously situated on the Elk River, 60 miles from Baltimore and the same distance from Philadelphia, and has a population of 500.

Going Down the Bay:

BIRDS-EYE VIEW OF ANNAPOLIS - SHOWING EASTPORT IN THE DISTANCE.

Birds-eye view of Annapolis looking towards Eastport and the bay.

But continue our course on the Chesapeake. After leaving the Chester and Magothy Rivers we next, on the western side, pass the brown lighthouse of Sandy Point. The country along the shore is beautiful, and shows marked signs of cultivation. Entering Annapolis Roads and passing Greenbury Point and Fort Madison we rapidly approach the quaint, old-fashioned city of Annapolis, the Capital of Maryland. This port has been the very appropriately called the "sleeping city." Even the arrival of a boatload of excursionists fails to rouse the inhabitants from their lethargy. Over every spot broods an air of quiet and antiquity. The old dark red, English bricks, and irregular streets seem to score the idea of "modern Improvement" as an innovation. The surrounds tell us plainly we are upon historic grounds.

Those old building once reflected the flames that consumed the "Peggy Stewart" . Here the Maryland Convention met in their early struggle for the Independence of the Nation. Most appropriate indeed it is to have the Naval Academy here that the future defenders of our country may be educated amid these patriotic memories. Annapolis was settled by Puritans. It was formerly called Proctor's Town and afterward Anne Arundel Town, but in 1708 received charter under the name of Annapolis.

The busy shipping of the Chesapeake Bay with all manner of vessels.

The Statehouse is near the center of the city and from it the streets diverge. The building is nearly two hundred feet high and commands a fine view of the surrounding country and forty or fifty miles of the bay. Annapolis is about thirty-five miles from Baltimore, has a population of 10,000, and is beautifully situated on the south bank of the Severn River. A visit to this picturesque city and a trip up the Hudson of Maryland to Round Bay, one of the magnificent steamers that so often leave our city for this retired resort, will amply repay itself.

Leaving Annapolis Roads on our trip further down the Bay, we pass what was formerly known as Tally's Point. Although naturally the most suitable site for a summer resort, it was not fully appreciated until a few months ago when "Chesapeake Steam Navigation and Hotel Company" made a survey of the place, and became fully convinced that with a few generous expenditures Tally's Point would become the most popular of all Baltimore Bayside Retreats.

Tally's Point, or Bay Ridge as it is now called, comprise a tract of land 146 acres in area, has all the advantages of the sea shore, and a hotel on a bluff seventy feet above the Bay. Lake Ogleton, a placid sheet of water, forms the western boundary of the property. This beautiful lake, which is entirely sheltered from the boisterous winds by magnificent woodlands, affords delightful boating and fishing for the more timid excursionists.

Avenues are being laid out; neat little cottages are being erected while summer houses, pavilions and other attractions of first-class summer resorts already enliven the place. Everything seems to tell us that the permanency of Bay Ridge is a matter of little doubt.

Music will be furnished during season by the Naval Academy Band. Distance from Baltimore: 28 miles; time, 2 hours.

Kent Island immediately opposite lies due west of Queen Anne's County. Kent Island is the largest island in the bay, being about 15 miles long. 'Twas here that the first white settlement in Maryland was made.

The soil being level, fertile and easily worked, fine and flourishing farms abound. Oyster dredging is an important source of employment.

Now we are nearing the beautiful but lonely lighthouse, (very much resembling Seven Foot Knoll, only the superstructure is white and lantern red) situated on a shoal new Thomas Point, at the mouth of the South River.

After passing the mouth of the West River and Horseshoe Point on the same side, we are opposite the entrance to the Eastern Bay, the southern boundary of Kent Island. A sail of about twenty miles up this inland bay and the Miles River, and St. Michael's River, St.

Michael's, an attractive little town fifty-six miles from Baltimore, with nicely paved sidewalks, street lamps and numerous religious and educational institutions. Out of the population of 2000 persons the stranger finds numerous kindly disposed and courteous natives. Fruit, oysters, and fish abound, making St. Michaels a delightful resort for excursion parties and visitors for a longer period. Shipbuilding is becoming quite an important industry in this sprightly retreat.

Eight miles southeast of Horseshoe point, on the Anne Arundel shore, is the beautiful and fashionable resort known to all Baltimoreans as Fair Haven. Fair Haven is delightfully situated near the mouth of Herring Creek. On account of the shallowness of the channel, the boat approaching or receding from the wharf has to chart a difficult course.

This course thus affording a fine opportunity to a few acres of the surrounding undulating, though cultivated farmlands. The Hotel is a large building with accommodations for numerous guests who find here nearly all the attractions of the seashore. A few bath-houses have been erected.

After passing Holland Point and Hog Island, we become conscious that we are fast receding from the familiar shores of dear old Anne Arundel. But our sadness is soothed by the thought that noble little Calvert will take its place.

Calvert County, is one of the smallest in the State, being but 32 miles in length, averaging about 7 mile in width and containing only 235 square miles. Tripoli, an excellent polishing material, is found in large deposits on the Patuxent River. The soil is soft, somewhat clayey and well adapted to the growth of corn, tobacco, and wheat. Immense quantities of fish and oysters are shipped to Baltimore and northern markets. This county extends along the bay for thirty miles.

A sail of six miles after the shore of Anne Arundel will bring the traveler abreast of a hexagonal, screw pile lighthouse, built in 7 ½ feet of water. This building is near the north end of Sharp's Island and marks the entrance to Choptank River. It has a brown foundation, white superstructure, and brown roof.

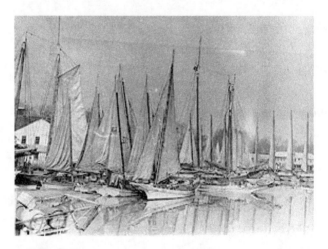

Cambridge, Maryland, oyster skipjack fleet. Maryland Archives.

Excursionists are continually leaving Baltimore, which after taking the same course, we have followed, enter the fair and beautiful Choptank River, and after a sail of nearly twenty miles arrive at the county seat of Dorchester, otherwise, Cambridge. Dear antique Cambridge! How interesting is the architecture of many of her houses, the material of which we learn, in many cases, was brought from the Old World. However, she is rapidly becoming modernized and is growing faster than any other Eastern Shore Town. Her excellent facilities for transportation, together with the industry of her inhabitants are the keynotes to her success. The town is illuminated by gas and has been incorporated. Formerly, a beautiful grove of willow trees enhanced the beauty of the ground surrounding the court-house, where excursionists enjoyed the cool shade and refreshed themselves with a draft from a delightful spring. But, alas! A hurricane in 1876 swept over Cambridge and dealt death and destruction to the magnificent grove.

Population 3,000; distance from Baltimore 72 miles.

If we had entered the Third Haven River, a short distance from the Choptank, we would, ere this, have arrived at the flourishing little town of Oxford. This beautiful and attractive retreat is situated on the east bank of the Tred Avon River or (Third Haven) River and is about 8 miles distant from the mouth of the Choptank. It has a population of over 500 and is one of the most important places in Talbot County. The surrounding country shows marked signs of cultivation, and the soil is fertile. Oxford is a very pleasant watering-place and summer resort. The swift and ever popular steamer Saml. J. Pentz has, for a few years past, been making attractive trips to this flourishing little village. The Hotel, known as the River View House, has recently been refitted and newly furnished, affording agreeable accommodations for those wishing to stay for a longer period at this desirable resort.

To resume our trip on the Chesapeake, probably the first thing of peculiar interest after leaving the vicinity of Sharp's Island will be Cove Point Lighthouse.

Point Lookout Hotel, Chesapeake Bay

A ride of four miles farther south and we are opposite the mouth of the Patuxent River, the southern boundary of Calvert County. Slowly we leave the fair banks of Calvert behind us and a sharp cape called Cedar Point introduces us to the most ancient county of

Maryland, called St. Mary's. The soil is slightly hilly and undulating, but as we proceed southward, it becomes low and level. Tobacco and corn are the principal crops.

After sailing for about fifteen miles, we pass Point-No-Point and four miles farther Point Look-In.

Soon we are at the famous watering place, called appropriately, Point Lookout, as the extremity of which is a lighthouse. The light is white and on the keeper's dwelling, which is also white with a red roof to the lantern.

On the same side, we have now the entrance to the beautiful Potomac River the southern boundary of Maryland, and the marine highway to the National Capitol. Here the Chesapeake is about 15 miles wide, we now have on our left a large island known as Smith's Island, behind which is the Tangier Sound.

Gradually the shores of Maryland recede, and the sunny banks of Virginia meet the eye. Smith's Point Lighthouse is the name of a screw-pile structure in twelve feet of water on a shoal east of the entrance to the Potomac. Almost immediately, opposite is the mouth of the Pocomoke River and the commencement of the sound of the same name. After passing Windmill and Stingray Points on our right, we command a fine view of the entrance to the Rappahannock River.

Cherry Point and a small town called Matthews are passed on the same side; while on the opposite bank is the beautiful little town of Eastville. A ride of a few miles brings us near the historic York River. Yorktown, the site of the surrender of Cornwallis to Washington, is on the south bank of this river, at not great distance from its mouth. But our vessel glides swiftly along and we can linger no longer on thoughts of the interesting Revolutionary War era struggle.

Fortress Monroe, prominently situated near the eastern extremity of Old Point Comfort, is in a short time reached. It did considerable service during the late war, but its history is so well known that it needs no further comment here.

Steamboat Louisa is running from Baltimore to Fort Monroe, Va.

Though passing somewhat hurriedly the largest military post on the Atlantic Coast, we will linger a little longer on the other attractions of Old Point Comfort.

In the early part of the 17th century, Captain Newport, driven by a severe storm, sought refuge in the waters of the Chesapeake. Appreciating the refuge he found behind the friendly cape; he named it Point Comfort.

If, as we have just said, it could be appropriately called so flattering a name two hundred and fifty-four years ago, how much more richly does it deserve so honorable a title now with his magnificent hotel, bath-houses and Government improvements?

Probably the principal attraction at present of Old Point Comfort is the Hygeia Hotel, a well conducted and very capacious summer and winter resort.

Nearly in the middle of the bay is Fort Wood, more well-known as the Rip-Raps. The fort is now used as a Government Arsenal.

The Monitor Passaic

Knowing that many of our readers will be enroute for the cozy little City of Norfolk, we will take a cursory view of that promising place and its marine approaches.

After leaving Old Point Comfort, we enter Hampton Roads, the site of the most important naval engagement fought during the late war, a brief sketch of which may prove of interest to our readers.

On the morning of March the 8th, 1862, the Confederate frigate, known as the *Merrimac*, steamed into Hampton Roads. This vessel had been formerly the finest in the service of the United States, but when the Navy Yard at Norfolk was abandoned, the Confederates gained possession. Determined to make her the "Monarch of the Seas," they razed her deck and fitted a sloping roof, plated with four and a half inch iron, until she at last presented the appearance of a floating fort.

Slowly the *Merrimac* steered towards the sloop-of-war, *Cumberland*, pouring with wonderful rapidity her huge cannon balls at that ill-fated vessel, whose gallant crew struggled bravely to defend her against the terrible and almost incessant fire. A hopeless task, indeed, for but a few hours afterward the *Cumberland* sank beneath her waves.

But in the beautiful language of Longfellow –
Next morn as the sun rose over the bay,
Still floated our flag at the main-mast head.
Lord, how beautiful was Thy day!
Every waft of the air was a whisper of prayer.
Or a dirge for the dead.

Sunday morning had hardly dawned when the *Merrimac* returned from Norfolk Harbor, expecting an easy victory over the remainder of the Union fleet. Steering directly for the *Minnesota,* she was startled by the appearance of a queer little vessel, was the invention of Captain Ericsson and called the *Monitor*.

A terrific engagement ensued, in which the plucky little "Yankee Cheese-box" , as the *Monitor* was contemptuously called, proved too much for the huge iron monster, which being somewhat damaged steamed back to Norfolk.

Upon entering the Roads, probably the first thing to attract our attention will be the magnificent edifice and grounds of the Soldiers Home, situated near which is the Normal Academy and Agricultural School for the education of Indian and Colored persons.

A beautiful but lonely lighthouse painted white and situated in deep water marks the extremity of Hampton Roads.

Here the waters of the James and Elizabeth Rivers mingle with those of the Chesapeake. Taking a southerly direction we enter the latter, beautiful river.

After passing Craney Island on our right, our attention is attracted on the same side of the river by the handsome grounds and fine building of the Marine Hospital, while on the other side we pass Fort Norfolk, and have a fine view of the new Cotton Factory. The town on our right is called Portsmouth and is a very thriving little city of nearly 20,000 inhabitants.

Opposite Portsmouth is Norfolk, " the future metropolis of Virginia."

Norfolk, was settled in 1683, incorporated as a borough in 1738, and became a city February 13, 1845. About 800 acres are embraced at the present time within the city limits. It is delightfully situated on the Elizabeth River, 8 miles from its mouth, is said to have the finest harbor in the United States, and has a climate unsurpassed by any city on the Atlantic Coast.

Had we continued our course on the Chesapeake, we would have passed a beautiful new resort known as "Ocean View" . This delightful watering-place is but a short distance from Norfolk and may be reached either by railroad or carriage. It has a magnificent beach and looks out upon the ocean through the capes.

The rough and rugged promontories at the entrance of the bay were named Cape Charles and Cape Henry by Captain Newport in honor of the two sons of King James.

Fifty-five or sixty miles from the capes, the Gulf Stream flows, aiding the "Merry Mariner" and exerting its wonderful influence over the climate of Eastern America and Western Europe.

Now having reached the boundless Atlantic, we fully realize that:

"We have left the still earth for the billows and breeze.
'Neath the brightest moons on the bluest of seas,
We have music, hark! Hark! There's a note over the deep,
Like the murmuring breath of a lion asleep,
There's enough of bold dash in the rich foam of the waves;
But yet there's a sweetness about the full swell,

CHESAPEAKE 1880

like the song of the mermaid – the chords of the shell,
Oh! Well, may our spirits grow wild as the breeze,
Beneath the brightest of moons on the bluest of seas!"

Using tongs for pulling up oysters from an oyster bar in Chesapeake Bay.

KEN ROSSIGNOL

Chapter One
Wawaset

It was a dark and stormy night on the Chesapeake as the new *Captain Douglas* steamed south out of Baltimore on the way to Washington. The sparkling new steamboat, the pride of the fleet, had left Baltimore in bright sunshine and as the day wore on the weather turned dangerously bad.

At over 250 feet in length, the *Captain Douglas* was one of the largest steamboats working the Bay and clearly was the finest. Even with the power of its engine and a wide beam, the ship was being tossed by the heavy seas. Capt. William Douglas, a grandson of the storied captain for whom the ship was named, was not only the president of the steamship company but was on board and in the wheelhouse. The winds weren't quite at gale force, which would have forced the *Captain Douglas* to seek shelter in the closest port. The winds were just under that level and had even slowed down a bit as the ship passed Point Lookout, Maryland at the mouth of the Potomac River and neared Smith Point, Virginia. After stopping on the Virginia side at Port Kinsale, the *Captain Douglas* began to work its way north up the Potomac, stopping at landings on both sides of the river.

Just as the weather began to clear, the wind die down, and the sun began to appear on the east horizon; another fireball grew bright to the west of the *Captain Douglas*. The officer of the watch at the wheelhouse helm sent the cabin boy to wake Capt. William as he ordered the helmsman to turn the ship in the direction of what could only be a ship on fire, the great dread of any captain of any vessel.

The *Captain Douglas* came within a half mile of the burning ship as Capt. William ran to the wheelhouse. The general alarm bell was sounded to awaken all the crew who may have been sleeping, and lifeboats were readied to be launched. The *Captain Douglas* was soon near the burning ship, which they could make out from the name on the hull was the *Wawaset*. Some passengers and crew had already jumped overboard, and only one lifeboat had been managed to be launched while two others were fully engulfed in flames. Capt. John Midgett had maneuvered the *Captain Douglas* on the side of the burning *Wawaset* to which the wind was not blowing. The captain ordered the lifeboats launched to fish the swimming passengers and crew of the *Wawaset* out of the waters of the Potomac off of Chatterton's Landing.

Within a half hour, the *Captain Douglas* had rescued the survivors who had jumped clear. A large fire hose had been hooked to a powerful pump to attempt to douse the flames that were rapidly eating away at what was left of the *Wawaset*.

An ungodly sound emitted from the hold where a bull and several cows had been contained as the animals simply roasted alive, bellowing their misery to the world. As the flames moved to the bow, having consumed most of the superstructure of the aft end of the steamboat, three men rose from a forward door of the saloon, without any life vests and began screaming to be saved. The seas had mercifully evened out as the wind died down, and the lifeboat from the *Captain Douglas* was able to get close enough to the burning ship to allow the three men to leap aboard to escape death.

At that point, the lifeboat had six crewmen from the *Captain Douglas* aboard rowing and fifteen people rescued from the *Wawaset.* The lifeboat crew rowed to the side of the *Captain Douglas* and passed the survivors up to many waiting hands who lifted them to the deck.

More screams erupted from the *Wawaset,* and the morning air was pierced by the wailing of a man who was fully on fire, his skin and clothes burning as the poor soul jumped into the water. The lifeboat crew quickly rowed to his aid, but he was gone when they arrived at the spot they had seen him enter the water. More cries for help came from the forward part of the *Wawaset* that while smoky, had not yet burned. A group of women and children, all in their bedclothes, huddled at the bow, waving and crying. Again the lifeboat crew worked to get back to the front of the ship and rescue them while the *Wawaset* lifeboat that had managed to get away unloaded another dozen survivors to the *Captain Douglas.*   Appearing from nowhere, it seemed; eight women and four children were packed into the lifeboat.

By the time the last person was saved from the wreckage of the *Wawaset* and fished out of the water, an amazing sixty-eight passengers and twelve crewmen. The crew said the conflagration had started with one of the engines that had caught fire and then the boiler exploded. They all watched from the deck of the *Captain Douglas* as the *Wawaset* finished burning, and the remainder of the hull simply sank. Its smokestack, paddle wheel and parts of the superstructure still appeared above the water line. The captain had made every attempt to run the steamer ashore when he realized that it was futile to attempt to fight the fire. Its position was recorded in the logbook of the *Captain Douglas* and the ship, at that point, was closer to Washington than any other major city, so it continued at top speed to that port. On board, *Captain Douglas* were twenty-five survivors and the bodies of ten who were recovered from the river.

The gruesome story of the burning ship was soon told in the *Washington Herald* after the first survivors had arrived in Washington.

Oyster can collection of Pat Buehler in St. Leonard, Maryland. *The Chesapeake Today photo*

Chapter Two

Cash is King

My younger brother William had only wanted to be a steamboat captain, just like our grandfather; instead he made an excellent president of the Norfolk & Baltimore line. As the president of the line, he assigned himself various runs at the helm in order to stay in touch with the business. Doing so kept him from being a prisoner in the main office which he had removed from Norfolk to Baltimore.

The adventure of going to sea continued to attract our growing clan. Two of my sons, the two oldest, both in the family tradition, were working as news readers on William's steamboats each summer. Molly was very strict and refused to let either Allen or Jack miss any days in school to be able to sail on the ships. Therefore, the very day that school let out in the spring, both boys had their bags packed and were at the dock waiting for the next steamship to arrive.

Charles, my next oldest son, wasn't interested in being on a boat; his interest was in working with his uncle's newspaper in Washington, D.C. The sirens and clanging bells of the fire trucks and following reporters around chasing murder stories were compelling to him. Molly let him go to work at the age of twelve on the condition that his Uncle John kept him on a short leash. The summers spent on the steamboat were more protected and predictable, and she didn't worry as much about Allen or Jack as she did Charles. He was supposed to be staying in the office or only leaving to chase news with his uncle; but the stories that he would tell his brothers when they arrived at the wharves in Washington indicated that far more exciting adventures were taking place.

Some of the news stories were taking place in bars and the back alleys of the capital city. Not knowing how much of the tales were just tall ones and how many were simply read from newspapers caused great worry. Thus a stream of reminders to his uncle about his welfare were made by both me and Charles's mother.

Captain Cullison was nearing his eighty-fifth year and was still as sharp as a tack. As my mentor in business, he had taken over my formal education where my grandfather had left off. I had been given my first job away from the *Savannah* by Capt. Cullison on one of his buyboats and then he had later hired me on as a captain.

From there, he then decided it was time to allow me to buy out his fleet of Chesapeake Bay buyboats. With the money plentiful from the business generated by the buyboats, all due to the bountiful supply of oysters, my wealth had steadily increased. The guidance from Capt. Cullison to invest in railroad stocks had been good, and all three railroads in which we both invested were prospering.

Baltimore Herald Building, Baltimore, Md.

My brother John had answered the siren call of the newspaper business and both Capt. Cullison and I had put up the money to allow John to operate his paper, making it one of the leading newspapers in the nation's capital.

At the ages of fourteen and sixteen, Jack and Allen were becoming well-known on the steamships for their entertainment and dramatic delivery of the news to the passengers.

On the times that I traveled on one of William's fleet of ships I listened to one of my boys regale the passengers on a steamer.

I not only marveled at how much the ships had changed from the old *Savannah*, but how much the news had changed as well.

I was also as proud as punch to see my sons excelling at reading the latest news to the passengers.

Doing so was a niche that had come about from my grandfather reading the paper to me; my taking up reading to passengers; and eventually kicking off the news reader position on most every ship on the bay. While the *Savannah* was a much smaller and simpler steamboat, the ones now plying the waters of the Chesapeake and Potomac were grand in every way.

The newspapers that the boys read to the passengers were also complicated as well as fascinating as the nation began the change to industrialization over the last 20 years. I was always glad that my sons had taken more to the newspaper and steamship business rather than the oyster and fishing business which was becoming more bloodthirsty every year.

While Capt. Cullison had grown his wealth to the point where he was one of the richest men in America; he continued to counsel me "cash is king, never forget it".

His advice was sound – he said to always to keep enough cash on hand to carry you for at least two years in case the banks founder or the stock market implodes. Neither of us had suffered during the various ups and downs of the markets since the end of the War Between the States.

While our Norfolk railroad investments suffered during the war, they bounced back as the nation began to heal and move ahead. Our other railroad stocks continued to gain as both the B & O and the

Pennsylvania were well run and tough competitors on the east coast as well as to the west to Chicago.

My seafood distribution business dominated the supply chain of oysters to most of the nation, as the New England oyster beds had been depleted. The oysters of the Chesapeake Bay were considered "white gold" and our buyboat fleet now numbered three dozens. They pulled in the lion's share of the oysters from all those out seeking them, illegally harvested or not; we bought oysters and paid cash.

The oyster pirates were out in force as Maryland and Virginia both put restrictions on the harvesting. Maryland stopped dredging unless by sail power and Virginia soon had to try to find ways to control the pirates from Maryland reaching down into Virginia waters at night.

Two attempts by Virginia Governor Cameron to crack down on the pirates had turned out to be ineffective. Maryland's oyster navy had run into pirates that fired on them, blasting them with cannon fire and from muskets.

Allen and Jack kept the passengers on *the Captain Douglas* and the *City of Baltimore* up to date on the latest news of the killings that took place on the Bay and the Potomac.

Capt. Cullison was right; cash was king and I stockpiled cash in a safe at home, in another one in the office, in safety deposit boxes at Mercantile Bank and with each of my brothers. I was not about to let a sudden run on banks turn my family back to the poor days of life in Georgia when we were kids after my father died.

Point of Rocks, Md. railroad station of the junction of the B & O Old Main Line and the Metropolitan branch.

Lore Oyster House, Solomon's Island, Md.
THE CHESAPEAKE TODAY photo

Chapter Three

- Paid by the Boom

Sean and Daniel Murphy had arrived in Baltimore on a schooner from the Caribbean with a load of spices bound for the McCormack warehouse. They had been working their way to America from Ireland by signing on any ship that would take them as seamen. A big night in a rough waterfront tavern for the two cousins had resulted in them both becoming very drunk. They thought they were going to be okay sleeping behind the bar in an alley if indeed any thought had been applied to the matter.

A horse-drawn cart with two figures approached the Murphy's as they lay snoring on top of trash piled behind the bar.

"Look at those two, Possum, they look pretty hardy, lets load them in the cart."

Possum and Nubby, his older brother, picked up Sean, who was a bit smaller than Daniel, and tossed him up into the rear of their horse-drawn cart that had been filled with straw.

"Ugh, this one is a big heavier, careful not to bang his head, we don't want to wake him," said Possum.

The two burly watermen loaded the two drunken seamen onto the cart and drove their borrowed rig down to the wharves.   They pulled up behind an oyster skipjack which was tied up in a row with about twenty other vessels.

"Deed-bye-Gawd, Cap'n, we have two more crew for ya," said Nubby, as the two burly watermen unloaded the two seamen who were still passed out as the first rays of the rising sun came over Baltimore.

Capt. Sam Bounds scratched his belly and spat a big wad of tobacco over the side of the boat into the harbor.

"Good work, boys that makes four new crewmen today, that's enough for this trip; now get yourselves aboard and let's shove off."

As the morning wore on, the heat from the sun awakened the two drunks as they lay out on the deck of the skipjack that was heading out the Patapsco for the open waters of the Chesapeake Bay.

"Who turned on the lights," said Sean rubbing his eyes and then kicking Daniel to wake him when he realized they were sailing down the river.

"Wake up, my dear cousin, it's a brand new day and somehow our alley we chose to bed down in is on the move."

"Sean, what the hell is going on?"

"I think we must have fallen asleep on someone's deck, mate. We ought to be more careful where we decide to lay our heads for the night," said Sean as he checked to make sure he still had his wallet and watch. Assured he still had possession of his valuables and his pay from their last job, Sean took a look around at the skipjack on which they were traveling and then at the coastline they were passing.

A bucket of seawater came crashing down across them, splashing across their faces and bringing them to a stark realization of their surroundings.

"Well, you two finally decided to wake up, have you?" said Capt. Bounds. "We have work to do. Go down to the galley and get yourselves some vittles. You're going to need to get some fire in your bellies for the work we have ahead."

"Begging your pardon, but we weren't looking for work just yet, we only yesterday got to Baltimore and wanted to look around a bit," said Sean.

"You signed up with us last night and we darn near didn't find you in time to sail, I had to send two men out looking for you, but lucky for you, we found you and now it's off to work we go," said Capt. Bounds with a hearty laugh. "You both claimed you were fit and able to work a long day; we'll soon find out if it was the whiskey talking or that you can carry your load."

E.C. Collier skipjack under sail. Photo credit Chesapeake Bay Maritime Museum St. Michael's, Md.

The hours turned into days and the days in two weeks. Sean and Daniel Murphy had become accustomed to the strange ways of Capt. Bounds as he sailed the *Peggy Stewart* from one oyster bed to another. Sean and Daniel worked the big dredge rig and quickly learned the system for culling the oysters by size, sending the smallest ones back overboard into the Bay and loading the keepers into bushels which were stored in the hold.

Long days and cold winds quickly weathered them and made them swear they would never again hire on a job while they were drunk. Capt. Bounds had promised them that as soon as the hold was full of oysters that they would return to Baltimore where they would be paid as soon as the wholesale agent accepted and paid for the cargo.

Finally at the end of the second week on the Bay the hold was full of oysters and Capt. Bounds made way for Baltimore.

"Sean you and Daniel can go forward now and fetch yourselves a jug of moonshine." Captain Bounds pointed to a forward hatch cover which contained the treasured liquor.

"Do you want me to bring you a jug as well," volunteered Sean.

"Yes lads, I expect I would like some to help my aching bones."

Sean looked at Daniel and winked.

"I'll bet an hour never passes that the captain hasn't tossed down a swig or two."

The two brothers started across the deck to retrieve the jug of liquor when the captain suddenly reached out and cut the line which held the ship's large boom and allowing the massive timber to sweep across the deck with great force. Sean and Daniel never saw it coming, and the boom swept them off the deck and into the cold water of the Bay.

Capt. Bounds and his two mates, both of them his sons, laughed as the *Peggy Stewart* sailed north up the Bay.

"They were hard workers; we are going to miss them boys, but I expect you and Nubby can find us a couple more behind the bar in a couple of days."

"Aye, captain and you will make sure they are paid by the boom as well."

Oyster dredging in the Chesapeake Bay. Library of Congress

Chapter Four
New Opportunities

I met Capt. Cullison at the Willard Hotel as he had asked. The nicest hotel in Washington, the Willard was around the corner from the White House on a prominent spot along Pennsylvania Avenue. Boasting the finest accommodations in the city of Washington, D.C. the Willard also had what many said was one of the grandest ballrooms and restaurants outside of New York.

When I entered the dining room lit by large chandeliers and paneled in black walnut, I saw that Capt. Cullison had a table at the rear of the room. When I approached his table, he was enjoying his daily glass of whiskey whilst he read the latest edition of the *Washington Herald*.

He motioned to me to sit down and got right to the point of our meeting.

"Do you remember when the Old Bay Line freighter *New Jersey* burned and sank in the shipping channel in the Bay back in 1870?"

I thought for a minute and recalled the incident.

"She went down and her crew was rescued from their lifeboats by oyster boats. Not a soul was lost."

"That's the one, Ethan. The *New Jersey* was one of the first steam packets with a propeller instead of a paddlewheel. They never did pinpoint the cause of the fire but since the ship was all wood, there was plenty of fuel for her to burn up. The replacement for the *New Jersey* was built of iron. Now all ships will be built of iron. We will soon see the day that all ships will be propeller driven. I think it's time we looked into buying passenger and freight lines on the North Atlantic routes; the more people want to come here from Europe, the more ships are needed to handle the trade."

"What does all that have to do with the *New Jersey*?

"We need to invest in the insurance companies too. The *New Jersey* was built in 1862 but was wooden, and was insured for $30,000. The cause of the fire was never assessed but the barrels of petroleum on board made sure the ship would burn, it was the first time such a cargo had been taken on by the Old Bay Line."

Steamship Dominion. Library of Congress

"Captain, are you suggesting it was arson?"

"I learned about it later, it was indeed arson but the insurance company had to pay off, there was no proof as the ship was down deep in the muck of the shipping channel. There were witnesses as to the fire, those who saw the fire and rescued the crew. The insurance paid for a new iron ship, the *Roanoke*, which went into service the next year, hauling freight from Norfolk to Baltimore. They built five more and made a lot of money."

"Aren't you a stockholder in the line?"

"Yes, but I was not privy to that information, not at the time; I found out about it last month. Anyone ruthless enough to defraud an insurance company will do it to their investors as well, that's why I want you to buy the Old Bay Line and by doing so, we will get rid of that Bailey fellow from Norfolk who runs it and protect my investment too. Ethan, I own forty-five percent of the stock, so that crook Bailey puts me at risk in a major way every time he pulls a crooked deal like that one. I would never have known if his accountant didn't tell me. I bought the accountant a new house to show my appreciation."

"Captain, I will do anything you ask me to do, you know that. Make the arrangements and let me know when we will complete the deal. However, I am also keen to become involved in overseas shipping as well."

"Ethan, there is one more investment we should undertake."

"What is that?"

"Insurance companies."

"If we go into that business as well, I hope we also engage the Pinkertons to protect us from the con-men like Thaddeus Bailey," I said.

"Ethan, I trust you will make sure that happens."

Baltimore American building in 1880 decorated for the 150th anniversary of Baltimore. Library of Congress

Chapter Five
Bloody Point

As the skipjack *Ellen A.* was sailing down the bay, Capt. Mortimer Tennyson spotted two men holding onto a channel marker at the mouth of the Eastern Bay just off Bloody Point.

Capt. Tennyson gently slid the *Ellen A.* alongside the buoy that allowed two of his crew to pluck the cold and nearly frozen lads from the grasp of death.

"Drag those lads down to the galley and let them warm by the stove," said Capt. Tennyson.

After an hour, the pair had thawed to the point that they could speak and Capt. Tennyson turned the helm over to one of his mates.

"Ay lads were you trying to swim across the Bay were ya?"

Daniel and Sean looked at each other and then Daniel spoke up

"Captain it must be the luck of the Irish for you to happen along today --- just in time I might add."

"We were makin' for home at St. Michaels when we spotted you boys hanging on for dear life. I'd say that you are truly lucky they have just started putting out the new buoys along the shipping channel. It sure gave you boys something to hang onto!"

Shivering from the frigid water of the bay, Sean spoke up.

"Cap'n we were finished from two weeks of oystering on the *Peggy Stewart* and heading back to Baltimore when the boom swept us overboard.

"Sounds to me like you were 'paid by the boom'! That ol' pirate Bounds has let off many a sailor with no pay, you were just lucky that he didn't slit your throat and throw you overboard --- that's' how Bloody Point got its name you know."

"If you lads are lookin' for honest work and real pay my boss is hiring, you can work for me for the next two weeks and after that it will be up to Capt. Douglas. He has the biggest fleet of buyboats on the Chesapeake and treats all of us like family."

"But I will warn you two Irish blokes drinkin' and workin' on a ship don't mix --- you might as well swim for that buoy back there if you think you'll be swillin' the rum on my boat."

"No worries about us getting into the rum again Cap'n; we have learned our lesson about the demon rum."

Culling oysters into compartments after being lifted from oyster bars on the floor of the rivers and Bay. Library of Congress

The next two weeks were hard work for the two young Irishmen. They operated the power rig and worked at culling the oysters pulled from the oyster bars below, tossing back the small ones and keeping the larger oysters filling the baskets.

The balmy October weather continued with Indian summer days and cool nights. Each time the skipjack holds were filled they offloaded their catch to one of Capt. Douglas's buyboats. That would take place every other day and kept the skipjack crew busy oystering instead of traveling back to Salisbury, Baltimore or Washington. The buyboats took care of getting their catch to the shucking houses and rail lines.

Sean and Daniel looked at each other and gave a quick reply to Capt. Tennyson, assuring him that he had nothing to worry about with them working on his boat.

Capt. Tennyson asked for the cook to bring him a fresh cup of coffee and a bowl of oyster stew, a daily occurrence on an oyster dredger. In his late sixties, the captain had achieved a senior status with the Douglas fleet. Standing a towering six foot four inches and with a rotund figure, he cut quite a figure in any port and had no trouble backing up his authority with force if need be.

With his red flame of hair belying his age, not a bit of gray, his beard was just as flamboyant, and he often told anyone who would listen that Blackbeard was his great-granddaddy. The truth of the matter is that he was a down-home tidewater gentleman who was known far and wide as being courteous to everyone he passed on the street and kind and caring to all of his crew and their families.

The two new sots on his boat soon learned much about Capt. Tennyson from the ship's cook. 'Old man Bones' had fed them plates of fried oysters and his famous oyster stew while he chuckled along with bits of history of life on the *Ellen A.*

"Perhaps, our luck didn't end with being saved from the cold," Sean told his brother. "From what the cook tells us, we couldn't find a fairer captain to crew for."

"Aye, Sean, perhaps we might want to behave for this boss and do things his way, our choices so far have landed us in cold water and nearly cost us our lives. This country is the land of milk and honey and perhaps it's time we took a sober approach to this new home in America."

"Daniel, I was thinking the same thing. If we break our backs for Capt. Tennyson, we might be able to get something out of life besides a hangover and dumped overboard."

14th Street Bridge over the Potomac River at Washington, D.C.

Steamer *Louise*

Chapter Six
Thanksgiving

The *Ellen A.* glided slowly into the dock at Cambridge and tied up for the new holiday of Thanksgiving. The Douglas fleet was ordered to take a break this year as the company was embracing Thanksgiving as a day of feast, prayer and thanks for the many bounties that the family had been given over the years. Now Ethan Douglas had given notice that the company would observe Thanksgiving, Christmas, New Year's Day and Easter as paid holidays, along with the Fourth of July.

November had turned cold and harsh with ice beginning to form along the shores during the nights when the wind died down.

Capt. Tennyson looked across the wide Choptank River to the north and saw large formations of various waterfowl darkening the sky with occasional blasts of gunfire in the distance.

"Men, get everything tied down good and have a fine day off tomorrow, with pay of course," said Capt. Tennyson. "Bones, after you get everything stowed, bring those two Irish lads and come down to my house as you are all staying for dinner. We have plenty of room in our big old house as well as the carriage house and having you all there will assure me that you aren't hanging out in the bars or Rose's Place. Nothing good can come from a visit there."

"Yessiree," said Bones, "I was worrying about if these two would ever make it back to work if they had a chance to linger at Roses."

Sean and Daniel looked at each other.

"Well, you can knock me down, brother, he not only saved our lives, gives us work, but now takes us home for a holiday. What would Momma say about this?"

"She would say, don't act like a couple of damn fools and try to remember you were raised with manners and treat your hosts with respect."

Bones looked at them and chuckled.

"When you see the granddaughters of the Cap'n, you will only begin to realize your good fortune. But if you get outa line in the least way you will get a lesson in keelhauling."

"Bones, I can only guess what that means so I will save you the trouble," said Daniel "We will only have the best of manners in our benefactor's home."

***

The next morning Bones woke Sean and Daniel from their slumber in loft of the carriage house.

"Come on boys you will be helping in the kitchen today as I am a cook for the day here as well, and I require your services."

Sean and Daniel looked around the loft over the top of the carriage house where they had spent the night and realized that Bones had brought them a steaming pot of coffee and two cups.

■■■

"Get a move on boys. First you are going to walk down to the river shore with those shotguns over by the stairs and bring in a couple of fat geese for today's dinner. Then you are going to be plucking and shucking for the rest of the morning. Get a move on -- times a wasting and we need to get those birds stuffed with oysters and in the oven before noon."

■■■

"Bones knows how to make us feel right at home with plenty of orders on a holiday morn; just like Momma used to do."

Bones heard Sean's remark to Daniel and stuck his head back in the door.

"We are having important company for dinner today and you will be meeting Capt. Douglas and his family who are joining Capt. Tennyson for the big day. Get moving lads," said Bones as he slammed the door on his way back to the main house.

The cold November morning air made for a quick way to wake up for Sean and Daniel. They toted the shotguns down to the edge of the Choptank and took a position in a duck blind along the shore. Capt. Tennyson's dog Brownie knew his job and tagged along. The big Chesapeake Bay retriever was ready for a quick workout that he knew would end with some prime fixings later that day. The morning hunting expedition was a joyful exercise for a vigorous dog like Brownie.

The first flight of geese flew in too high, and their shot missed. Even Brownie seemed to flinch at the poor skills of the new hunters. But dogs are loyal not only to their master but to the hunt itself and they are patient as well.

■■■

The next crew of honkers flew lower, and the sky continued to darken with great masses of Canadian geese. This time both Sean and Daniel each brought down a large bird and Brownie quickly went out about twenty-five feet from shore and retrieved them one bird at a time.

The large manor house had a big back porch which was just right for plucking birds and shucking oysters. That was just what the two new crewmen for the *Ellen A.* were doing for the next two hours.

■■■

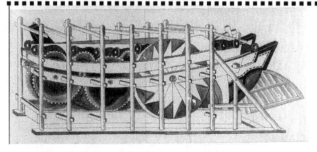

Side wheel mechanism of a paddle wheel.

Trading tales of being home in Ireland while downing big steaming mugs of hot chocolate brought out to them by the colored maid kept the two working hard. Before long they were about to present Bones with two finely plucked geese and a large pail of freshly shucked oysters.

Capt. Tennyson appeared on the porch with Bones and greeted the two guests.

"Well lads, Bones tells me that you have decided to join us today as our guests. I have to say it's mighty considerate of you both to join in with the preparation."

"Cap'n tis an honor to join you here for this day," said Daniel.

As Bones supervised the preparation of the oyster dressing being used to stuff both of the big geese; Alice the maid, worked at a counter chopping up celery, onion and spices while an iron skillet cooked up a mess of bacon. Once the bacon had cooked down, Alice added in the celery, onion, and spices.

Bones put both stuffed geese in the oven in the large kitchen and turned to Sean and Daniel.

"You fellows have done a good job today, but I can't let you sit down to dinner with proper folk," he said with a wink.

Sean and Daniel both looked at each other as the disappointment spread over their faces.

"Ha lads do you really think we would make you eat a bowl of hash on the back porch? Go get yourself a bath and get clean clothes on and after you have gotten presentable you will represent the Murphy clan and will join us in the dining room and not a minute earlier.
    ***

CHESAPEAKE 1880

The arrival of Capt. Ethan Douglas and his family in a coach at the front door set the Tennyson household buzzing. With Capt. Douglas and family a total of ten guests joining the table and the Tennyson family, another twelve, plus the two Murphy brothers that made twenty-four plus Bones and Alice, who always joined the elaborate dinner as well. Plates of sweet potatoes, green beans, hot apple pies as well as collard greens and kale accompanied the two fine roasted geese. The oyster stuffing made the day.

For Sean and Daniel Murphy the opportunity to meet the president of the company and his daughters were enough to have them observing their best manners.

***

I saw the promise that the Murphy boys possessed and that Capt. Tennyson had found in them. Solid and soon-to-be-sober as well types were just what was needed on the water to make the business work. I also watched as my daughters Phyllis and Louise smitten with the two brothers.

Capt. Tennyson led us in prayer and thanked the Lord for our blessings as we had many to be grateful. We all began with oyster stew and then Capt. Tennyson carved the big birds and the feast began.

As Capt. Tennyson related the events of the past two weeks from the time he had found the two nearly drowned and frozen river rats to their hunting prowess of the morning; I could tell that the Murphy boys were going to have a role in my company in the days ahead. And given the way my daughters were acting at the dinner table these young men might be around a lot longer than this meal.

"What plans do you men have here in Maryland?" I asked.

"Capt. Douglas, we have worked on four different ships in order to cross the ocean and to get to America and each time we left a paycheck behind. Your boat, the *Ellen A.*, with Capt. Tennyson, is the only one to have treated us fair, not to mention saving our lives," said Sean. "We would beg that you consider keeping us on permanently."

I considered his words and saw Capt. Tennyson grin and wink with a nod of his head.

"Men, your captain, and Bones both believe you have the right qualities to make a good crew and show promise well beyond that level. Be sober, be on board at the right time and be honest and you both shall have jobs as long as you want them."

I could see from the expressions on the faces of my daughters and wife that they were pleased with the direction of the conversation. As my daughters were both now past twenty, the idea of courting time approaching was worrisome to me, but I knew it to be inevitable. That our company may be taking on two capable men was always good news given the scalawags and pirates who populated the docks and wharves of the Chesapeake looking for work.

After dinner, we learned that Sean and Daniel could both play the fiddle and 'cut the rug' as the night wore on. I also learned that my daughters both liked to dance as well, especially with the two young men now new in their lives.

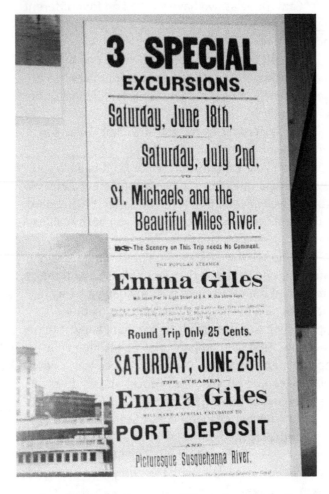

Display of Steamboat memorabilia at Chesapeake Bay Maritime Museum, St. Michaels, Md.
THE CHESAPEAKE TODAY photo

Chapter Seven
Virginia's raid on oyster pirates

The oyster wars continued to rage on the Chesapeake Bay in the winter of 1881 as competition between Virginia and Maryland watermen often turned to gunfire.

Tough times had settled on Virginia during reconstruction, and the Commonwealth had to sell its fleet of police boats. The intrusion of Maryland oystermen into Virginia waters grew to the point that Gov. Cameron had to act. Being without any state patrol boats, he ordered the state militia onto a fleet of vessels composed of tug boats, small work boats, a few skipjacks and one old steamer. The Governor armed the fleet with a few small cannon and rifles and then set out to arrest the Maryland pirates.

Oyster Police battle oyster pirates of the Chesapeake Bay.
Library of Congress

The first shots fell far short of their mark as the cannons mounted on the bow of an old tugboat blasted towards the Maryland pirates. The shot was convincing to the intended targets who quickly raised a white flag of sorts. Other boats followed suit while a dozen or more fled as fast as they could manage.

At the court proceedings the next day, with justice being swift in Hampton Roads, forty-two captains were sentenced to ten years in prison for violating Virginia harvesting regulations. The judge noted the compassion the law held for working men and reduced the sentences to one year, holding that the men needed to heed the law and return to caring for their families.

After a barrage of newspaper articles and petitions from Maryland, the Virginia Governor soon exercised a rarely used power of pardon and let all of the pirates out of jail after one month.

Now the Virginia newspapers were roundly criticizing Gov. Cameron for failing to hold the Maryland watermen accountable. Worse yet, a month after being released from jail, the lot of them were back at work illegally harvesting oysters in Virginia waters.

Gov. Cameron once again assembled a fleet of vessels and hoping to counter the bad press he took over setting the pirates free, he even included several newspaper reporters for another raid on the pirates.

The appointed time arrived, and militia, officials, and reporters all boarded the assembled flotilla of small craft.

Gov. Cameron, accompanied by his Militia Commander, Gen. Sam Mosby, son of the famed Confederate raider, stepped onto the deck of the tugboat *Night Heron*.

The *Night Heron* was one of the working tugs of the Old Bay Line and Capt. Joe Greenwell was at the helm, accompanied by his son, Joey.

"Pop, shall I get some coffee for the Governor and General?"

"Good idea to be cordial to our guests, especially paying ones," replied Capt. Greenwell.

As the fleet of vessels began to make its way north on the Chesapeake, the night was clear.

The wind began to pick up, churning up the waves into three to four feet high, giving the boats a rough going.

"Pop, I see lights ahead off of Smith Point, between the light and the point, right over the top of the oyster bar," reported Joey.

Gen. Mosby, along with the Governor and two aides were also crowded into the wheelhouse.

"Let's give them a shot across their bow to show them we mean business," Mosby ordered his aides.

"Yes sir," replied one aide who opened the door to the deck and immediately hit with a shrieking blast of wind which tossed the lanterns sideways.

The aide went to the gun crew on the bow of the tugboat and ordered them to fire near the closest oyster pirate.

All of the pirate boats in the distance were designated due to being in violation of rules requiring them to tong and dredge for oysters only during daylight hours.

As the first shot and then several others fell far short of the area near the pirates, the noise of the cannon got their attention.

***

"Those crazy Virginians are after us again, Roscoe," Capt. Boogey Poe said with a laugh. "I am tempted to shoot back but I'm afraid we'd hit one of the fools. They are out of range to hit us, and if they give us chase across this bar, I'll bet we can lead them to shallow water and make them run aground."

"Captain, let's just make our escape back to St. George Creek and the safety of our shore, I had enough of that Virginia jail last time."

"Okay, Roscoe, we all lost money sitting behind bars and we will have no trouble outrunnin' them gummermint boats a'gin."

The wind howled even stronger and caught the sails of the sloop *Miss Aubrey* giving her a strong burst of speed up the dark Potomac.

She was quickly on the way to her home creek on the Maryland side of the river, safe from the gunboats of the Virginians.

As the *Miss Aubrey* took off with the wind, other pirates working the oyster bar at Smith Point laughed at the hapless Virginia Navy but followed the lead of Capt. Poe and also fled back to their safe harbors at Piney Point, Crisfield, and Smith Island.

Of several dozen pirate boats, only one, the *Palo Alto*, was captured with the Captain and Mate escaping in a rowboat.

In the meantime, one of the old freighters had a coal stove turn over and started a fire that caused several militiamen injury and the fire quickly extinguished. Of course, that was the vessel that was transporting the reporters, who not only got a good view of the poor marksmanship of the Virginia flotilla, but heard the laughing of the pirates. The overturned stove and the minor injuries only added to the story.

The next day and for a few days thereafter, the newspapers in Norfolk, Portsmouth, and Hampton Roads, all trumpeted the latest adventures of Gov. Cameron and his Oyster Navy. Worse yet, the Norfolk Academy of Music turned the event into a Comic Opera.

The pirates returned the next night knowing that it would be a long time before they would see the Virginia officials again and could take all the oysters they wanted, unimpeded by the lawmen.

After six hours of productive work on the Smith Point oyster bar, filling the hold of the *Miss Aubrey* to its maximum, Capt. Roscoe told his crew it was time to head back to port.

***

Capt. Joe Greenwell docked *Night Heron* at the steamboat dock in Norfolk next to the *CAPTAIN DOUGLAS,* which was in port for the night and set to leave at 10:00 am the next day. Capt. Greenwell went aboard and found that I was in my stateroom. Being an old acquaintance of my grandfather and namesake of my ship, it was like old home week to visit with Capt. Joe.

"I hope you charged the Governor plenty for this trip up the Bay," said Capt. Joe with a laugh. "They decided to use their toy cannon they had put on the bow of my boat and fired way too soon to hit anything, but the Maryland boys all got a good laugh, and I'm afraid we did too. They all got away, and that old tub *Marcy Jones* nearly burned up when the chop dumped the coal stove in the galley. And, Cap'n, we'll be reading about it for a few weeks as there were a half dozen newspaper reporters on board, to boot!"

"Perhaps, Capt. Joe, we won't charge anything at all, getting our bill for services rendered will be like rubbing salt in the wounds," I told him.

I learned a long time ago that dealing with the politicians of Maryland and Virginia was quite an art and curried favor with them made life easier for a business that depended upon the whimsical decisions of government officials.

Captain Joe Greenwell had been with the company since the days when I bought out Capt. Cullison's Buyboat fleet. He had been training his son at the helm of our buyboats, steamers and now a tugboat. Within a couple of years, Joey would be ready for a vessel of his own.

A 100-year-old buyboat's last days in Nomini Bay, Va. Photo from *The Chesapeake Today*.

Chapter Eight

An Office Seeker's Revenge

THE NEWS READERS:

Allen and Jack were once again on the *Captain Douglas* and honed their skills as news readers. With each passing day they were able to hop on board one of our ships of the Baltimore & Norfolk Line or Old Bay Line and entertain the passsengers. Meanwhile, they were one step closer to working with my brother John's newspaper as a career and further away from my transportation companies.

The summer of 1881 had been one of upheaval, something that our nation didn't need as the wounds of the War Between the States were still fresh.

On the 2nd day of July as President Garfield was shot as he and his two sons prepared to board a train to Massachusetts to join family members for the Fourth of July holiday, after first attending the commencement exercises of his alma mater, Williams College.

Baltimore and Potomac Railroad station where President Garfield was shot.

CHESAPEAKE 1880

The President was within seconds of entering the station of the Baltimore and Potomac Station in the capital city when just before boarding the 9:30 am *Limited Express;* a jilted office seeker grabbed for the glory of being an assassin when a job with the government had been denied him.

James Abram Garfield was an unwilling president drafted for the post by his Republican Party. A brilliant man.

***

"Ladies and Gentlemen, lend me your ears," began Jack as he stood next to the special podium used by the News Readers and ministers in Sunday travel.

"We have several news items for you from *The Washington Herald* and *The Weekly Register*. First, I will catch you up to date on the events that led to the President's current dangerous condition due to the dastardly work of an assassin."

PRESIDENT SHOT BY CRAZED SUPPLICANT
By John William Douglas
THE WASHINGTON HERALD
Washington, D.C. --- President Garfield was felled by two shots fired by an assassin today as he entered the Baltimore and Potomac Railroad Station for a trip north for the Fourth of July and a much-needed vacation.

Reports are that President Garfield's condition continues to be guarded, and doctors expect that it is possible he may not recover but are not giving up hope.

The President's assassin has been identified by Washington Police as Charles Julius Guiteau, 40, of Illinois and lately of this city. He had spent considerable time petitioning the government for a job and due to being suspected a lunatic was denied same.

Of several residents of the area who have had contact with Guiteau, the opinion shared among them is that he is erratic in the extreme about politics, moody and even insane.

The view of many upon hearing the news of the tragic shooting, just sixteen years after President Lincoln being shot dead, also in Washington, that the nation is over-populated by fanatics.

The question is being asked in some circles as to when Congress will appropriate funds for and establish a guard unit for the President.

Garfield had become President in an unlikely fashion and had never sought the nomination of the Republican Party. Instead, he had been nominated at last year's Republican Convention on the 36th ballot.

The convention had become split with the Stalwart faction of the Republicans supporting nominating President Ulysses S. Grant for a third term and the Half-Breeds favoring the nomination of Maine Senator James G. Blaine. After 33 ballots were cast at the Chicago Convention of the Grand Old Party, Grant was leading but had not attained a majority of the delegates needed for the nomination.

Garfield had been a dark horse, being a Civil War hero and nine-term Congressman and well thought of but never believed to harbor aspirations to be President.

With most of his support coming from the Half-Breeds, Garfield chose as his Vice-Presidential running mate, Chester A. Arthur, who was a Stalwart.

During the fall election, it is said that Guiteau had become a self-appointed political operative and was designated to speak to small gathering of black voters in New York on behalf of Garfield.

CHESAPEAKE 1880

Reports from staff at the White House reveal that Guiteau's sense of importance over that minor role in the campaign soon exceeded all boundaries of reality. He began to beseech the new Secretary of State Blaine with bids to be appointed to be Minister to France or Austria.

The latest report from the White House reveals that the President is in critical condition and that when shot at the train station, predicted his death to the attending physician.

Dr. D. W. Bliss told this reporter that he was told by a city health officer who was the first doctor on the scene that the words of the President were: "Doctor, I am a dead man."

Dr. Bliss conferred with ten other doctors about what to do to treat the President before adhering to the orders of the President to take him back to his bedroom in the White House, which they did in a police ambulance.

A Police official reports that when the assassin Guiteau was taken to jail he asked a police sergeant if he himself was a Stalwart; and when told that he was, Guiteau then offered to make him Chief of Police.

One of the President's friends said that Garfield was perhaps the last of the "log cabin presidents" raised from poor beginnings.

His father died when Garfield was only a baby and he had worked as a janitor and carpenter as he put himself through college.

President Garfield was known to have expressed exasperation at the role of the president to have to give visitation rights to all those seeking a job with the government, sometimes as many as one hundred in a day.

It is well known that Guiteau was one of those who spent countless hours waiting for a turn to seek a job even by appealing directly to the President one occasion.

***

After the President had been taken to the White House, a great storm of controversy over his care began to develop, particularly whether or not he was being given the most up-to-date treatment.

A British surgeon, Joseph Lister, had been advocating the use of antiseptics to battle germs as the only way to successfully treat those suffering from wounds and other ailments.

There were twelve doctors who had rushed to the train station and the White House to treat President Garfield.

John reported on the condition of the President.

Doctors Poked Germ Infested Fingers in President's Wounds; Will Kill Their Patient, Says Surgeon

By John William Douglas

THE WASHINGTON HERALD

Washington, D. C. --- A noted British surgeon has advocated the immediate treatment of the wounds of President Garfield with antiseptics to combat the spread of germs.

In addition, Dr. Joseph Lister told the Daily Mail that the physicians who have been treating the president are themselves killing him.

"For twelve doctors to have put their unwashed and germ-coated fingers in the president's wounds as they poked and prodded searching for the bullet fired into his back is outrageous," said Dr. Lister.

Every report shows that the president is deteriorating from infections caused not by a bullet but the doctors. It is the doctors who are going to kill him, said Lister and other physicians who advocate the use of antiseptics to kill germs.

The doctors who have been treating the President since the assassin fired twice as he entered the train station in Washington, believe that 'bad air' causes disease.

In order to improve the President, they are going send him on a special train to New Jersey to a friend's home on the coast to improve his health by breathing in fresh ocean air.

A special spur siding is being constructed to enable the train to arrive at the beachfront home of Charles Franklyn in Long Branch, New Jersey.

Meanwhile, the man who shot the President in part due to his delusions of grandeur and subsequent disappointment in not being named minister to France is awaiting trial.

Even though Charles Guiteau was secreted into a special cell with bulletproof door, he was the subject of an attempt on his life by a jail guard.

As if the story of the assassination of the President was not strange enough, noted inventor Alexander Graham Bell was brought to the White House. Prior to the president being moved to New Jersey, Bell was asked to use his new induction technology to attempt to find the bullet in the president's back. The attempt was unsuccessful, reports Bell.

It was later learned that Bell's attempt to find the bullet was thwarted by the unusual construction of the President's bed, in that it had metal springs.

***

As the weeks went by the President's condition worsened and on Sept. 19, 1981, Garfield died.

Afterward, his killer, whom many believed to be insane, boasted that, "Yes, I shot the President but his doctors killed him."

Charles Guiteau convicted of killing Garfield.

After the spectacle of a trial, which included the assassin joining in with his defense and calling his attorney's "blunderbuss lawyers" Guiteau was found guilty and sentenced to be hanged by the neck until dead.

The defense unsuccessfully mounted an effort to have Guiteau declared not guilty by reason of insanity and provided a long list of his lunatic claims.

The voir dire for the trial exhausted 175 potential jury members before twelve persons not believing that Guiteau should immediately be executed could be found. As it was, when the case went to the jury, it only took them one hour of deliberation to come back with a verdict of guilty.

The Washington Herald reported on each day of the trial with every day proving to more bizarre than the day before.

When Dr. Bliss, the chief physician who also performed the autopsy testified the scene became even more bizarre.

The doctor statement revealed that the doctors were probing the wrong side of the President's back the entire time they were treating him. Bliss used the actual spine of the President, that had been removed from his corpse, to show the damage done to him by the bullet.

When the prisoner was being taken back to jail after one day's testimony in the old Criminal Court Building in Washington when a horse pulled alongside the police van.

A drunk farmer named Bill Jones fired a shot at Guiteau which missed its mark but his cloak.

Guiteau offered his closing arguments and sang "John Brown's Body and called himself an American patriot.

After appeals to the courts and to President Chester Arthur had been exhausted, Guiteau was hanged on June 30, 1882.

***

The News Readers stayed busy all along the routes between Norfolk, Baltimore and Washington keeping passengers up to date on the latest news. Soon major railroads began to copy them, citing the service as being beneficial to those with poor eyesight, the illiterate and the elderly.

***

"Now this report from the *Weekly Register* of Point Pleasant, W. Va.: but before the news, these announcements are included for your edification and enjoyment," said Allen.

***

The Weekly Register,

Published Every Wednesday Morning, by **GEORGE W. TIPPETT,** Editor, and Proprietor. Office upstairs, Stortz's Block. Entrance on Main St.

KEN ROSSIGNOL

Terms of Subscription.

One copy one year, in advance $1 50

One copy five years, in advance 5 00

All papers discontinued as soon as time paid for expires and no subscriptions taken unless paid for in advance.

Advertising Rates

One square (one inch) one week, $1 00

Each additional insertion, .50

Fourth of Column twelve months, 25 00

Half Column twelve months, 50 00

One Column twelve months, DO 00

Cards not exceeding seven lines, 1 yr 8 00

Legal advertisements at the rates fixed by law.

Local notices 15 cents per line, the first insertion.

All advertisements for a shorter time than three months, considered transient.

Transient advertisements must be paid for in advance, to ensure insertion.

Yearly advertisements payable half yearly in advance.

Legal publications must be paid for, in all cases, before the delivery of the certificate of publication.

Personal publications and those recommending candidates for office charged regular advertising rates.

Marriage and Death notices, published free; but obituaries and tributes of respect, charged at half the usual advertising rates.

Announcements for office, for county, $5; State and District, $10 00; on regular ticket, $10 00.

ATTORNEYS.

JAS. W. HOGE, JAS. D. MENEGER, CHAS. K. HOGG
HOGE, MENAGER & HOGG,
Attorneys at Law, Point Pleasant, West Virginia, (Office in the Court House.) Practice in the counties of Mason, Putnam, Cabell, Roane and Jackson; in the Supreme Court of Appeals and the U. S. District and Circuit Courts, for West Virginia.

W. H. TOMLINSON & D.W. POLSLEY
TOMLINSON & POLSLEY,
Attorneys and Counselors at Law, Point Pleasant, West Virginia, practice in the County of Mason; the United States District Court for West Virginia and in the Supreme Court of Appeals of West Virginia.
Prompt attention given to the collection of claims entrusted to them. Address, Point Pleasant, W. Va.

J. A. GIBBONS,
ATTORNEY AT LAW. Point Pleasant, West Virginia, will practice in the U. S. District Court, in the State Supreme Court and the Circuit Courts of the 7th Judicial District; office located in the Court House.

JOHN E. TIMMS,
Attorney at Law and Notary Public, Point Pleasant, West Virginia. Will practice in the Courts of Mason and Putnam counties, and attend promptly to all business entrusted to him.

JAS. H. COUCH, JR.,
Attorney at Law and Notary Public, Point Pleasant, West Virginia, will practice in the counties of Mason and Putnam. All business will receive prompt attention.

W. R. GUNN,
Attorney at Law, Point Pleasant, West Virginia. Practices in the Courts of Mason County, the Court of Appeals of West Virginia and the United States District Court for this State. Prompt attention given to the collection of claims. Office near the Court House.

RANKIN WILEY, Jr.,
Attorney at Law, Point Pleasant, West Virginia. Practices in the County of Mason; the United States District Court for West Virginia, and in the Supreme Court of Appeals of West Virginia. Prompt attention given to the collection of claims.

JOHN W. ENGLISH,
Attorney at Law will practice in the Courts of Mason, Putnam, and Jackson, and in the Court of Appeals of West Virginia. Address Point Pleasant, Mason County, West Virginia.

PHYSICIANS

DRS. BARBEE & FRAVEL,
Northwest cor. 6th and Main Streets, Point Pleasant,

West Virginia. Office hours from 8 to 10 a. m. and 3 to 10 p. m.

W. R. NEALE, M.D.
OFFICE Main Street, between 2nd and 3rd; residence, Main Street, between 6th and 7th. Attends promptly to all calls, whether day or night. When not professionally engaged can always be found at his office.

DR. S. G. SHAW,
PHYSICIAN AND SURGEON, tenders his professional services to the public. Calls promptly attended to. Office, cor. Main and 3rd streets, opposite the old Presbyterian church.

DR. L. F. CAMPBELL,
PHYSICIAN and SURGEON, tenders his professional services to the citizens of Point Pleasant and vicinity. Can be found for the present at the Drug Store of E. J. Mossman.

TO THE LADIES.

DRESS TRIMMINGS
THE MISSES RISK wish to inform the citizens of Point Pleasant and vicinity, that they have in stock a full line of Dress Trimmings, such as Silks, Satins, Plain, Striped and Brocaded Velvets, Cords and Tassels, all kinds of Linings, Crinoline Wiggins, all kinds of Laces and Passementerie Trimmings. Those goods are all for sale LOW FOR CASH. Ladies please call and examine them. THE MISSES RISK.

"And now a news item about the wounded president," said Allen.

From the *Weekly Register:*

We met last week a lady of the family resident on Governor's Island. She told us that since July 2nd, when President Garfield was shot, General Hancock had refused to go to public dinners, or on those excursions of a quiet kind he is very fond to take. We could imagine gallant old General Pike Graham, of the Grahams of Virginia, making the point, but here we have it from General Hancock of Pennsylvania. "It is not proper that I should accept festive entertainments while the President, ex-officio my commander-in-chief, is hovering between life and death." Who will say the age of chivalry is past, when a Major General of the army, defeated by the lavish use of money in New York, thus holds himself toward the man that is President in place of himself?

***

"For those unaware of the recent political history of this nation, President Garfield narrowly defeated Gen. Hancock, the Democrat, in the election last fall," Allen explained to the passengers of the *CAPTAIN DOUGLAS* as the ship sailed down the Potomac on her way to the next landing.

"Now we shall note some other postings in the Sept 7, 1881 edition of the *Weekly Register*," Allen boomed across the Grand Saloon and began to recite:

Boss Snake Story.

We now positively believe that the serpent tempted Eve. Mrs. Van Aukeen, living near Lake George, was startled one day last week by the sight of a large rattlesnake making its appearance in her kitchen, where she was at work, and, seizing her by the skirt, tried to pull her toward the door. Woman's curiosity at last overcame her fear; she followed the snake down to the lake, where she was still more horrified to find her little daughter on the point of drowning. Seeing a little one fall into the water, it seems that the snake, with astonishing instinct, crawled to the house to give warning. The subtlety of the serpent thus established. – Ex.

Now, no doubt many incredulous people will not believe the above, but it is true, every word of it.

When a young man devotes fifteen minutes to arranging his necktie on Sunday evening, and brushes his hair with a little more particularity than usual, it is a sign that he has "pressing" business on hand, and will get into a tight squeeze before midnight.

In Baltimore, a fine of $1 is imposed for every oath used. A newspaper man on a princely salary would die a pauper in that city.

A Canada farmer discovered a Pit containing 500 skulls. Must have been the site of an ancient theater to have had so many deadheads in the pit.

It Cured Him

When I was a boy of about nine, a servant of my father's put a pipe into my mouth, assuring me that to smoke would make a man of me. I puffed away most vigorously and persevered till I became sick and fell on the floor. I have never smoked since. In much the same way, I was cured of hero worship. When I was a college youth, I ventured one day to call on a man of some eminence to whom I had been introduced. He received me with smiles and compliments, and as I left his presence I was ready to proclaim him the most gentlemanly man I had ever met with; but after I went out I lingered at the door a moment to determine whether I should call on another great man who lived near, and I overheard the polite gentleman I had left call his servant to administer to him the most terrible scolding I had ever listened to in my life for letting in that stupid, impudent stripling. – This cured me of hero worship and of interviewing great men. Since that date I have at times gone to a distinguished man's house with letters of introduction, and turned at the door for fear of what might come.

Home Manners

As man may indulge in many things, in the seclusion of his own family, which would be out of place anywhere else, he may put on his dressing-gown and slippers, and lay off in general, when there are no strangers present; but he should never forget the laws of decorum even at home. It is often said that you must live with a man to know him thoroughly, and it may be well for our reputation that we do not all live under the same roof. All our courtesies ought not to be reserved for public use. The habit of fault-finding and saying sharp and harsh words in the family circle grows upon one imperceptibly, and he may become a nuisance before he knows it. Good manners are a kind of lubricator that abates friction and keeps everything moving smoothly and pleasantly.

The Doll's Mission

The doll is one of the most imperious necessities, and at the same time one of the most charming instincts of female childhood. To care for, to clothe, to adorn, to dress, to undress, to dress over again, to teach, to scold a little, to rock to cuddle, to put to sleep; to imagine that something is somebody – all the future of woman is there. Even when musing and prattling, while making little wardrobes and little baby clothes, while sewing little dresses, little bodices, and little jackets, the child becomes a little girl, the great girl becomes a woman. The first baby takes the place of the last doll.

Temper a Good Quality.

Never marry a woman without temper. Some may consider this strange, but it will be found good advice. Temper is a good thing in a woman; for with the spirit which accompanies temper, always comes activity, energy, industry, a proper personal pride, and self-respect that, ensures honor and a good reputation. A woman without a temper may be amiable but will be likely to be more or less insipid, timid and irresolute. Steel and whalebone are both good qualities in a woman. A jack-knife isn't usually considered worth much without a good smart spring.

A missionary orator stood on a Sydney platform. Before him was a large audience, which included many daintily-mannered ladies. – He had to describe the 'customs' of certain savages, and, of course, everybody wanted to know how the darkies dressed. And this is how be put it: 'They had,' he said, 'only a single article of attire, and that was a fig leaf, which was still on its native tree, a quarter of a mile oft.' Having thus adroitly disposed of his difficulty, he passed on to more congenial topics.

The following is recommended as a sure cure for sleeplessness: Wet half a towel and apply it to the back of the neck, pressing it upward toward the base of the brain, and fastening the dry half of the towel so as to prevent too rapid exhalation. The effect is prompt and delightful, cooling the brain and inducing sweeter, and calmer sleep than any narcotic. Warm water may be used, though more persons prefer cold. To those who suffer from over-excitement of the brain, when the result of brain work or pressing anxiety, this simple remedy has proved an especial boon. We advise a thorough trial of it.

The seed dies into a new life so does man.

***

"Thank you for your attention for this portion of our voyage and after a brief intermission for a refreshing beverage, our News Reading will continue," said Allen. He ended that session of the News Reader with a bow and sweep of his hat to the polite applause of the passengers in the Grand Saloon of the *CAPTAIN DOUGLAS*.

***

CHESAPEAKE 1880

Chapter Nine

New Rails for Shore; Pier for Chesapeake Beach

Moving freight by sea and land had become the greater part of our business with the connections between the two filled with challenges and opportunity.

My family had grown to ten fine children with only the two youngest girls not yet married off. But I had hopes that before the year was over, they might be giving us the news that the two Irish lads they met at Capt. Tennyson's for Thanksgiving dinner had asked for their hands in marriage. The idea of both of them getting married at the same time to brothers was fine with me as I figured I could get away with paying for one shindig.

On a trip to New York with Capt. Cullison to attend a stockholder's meeting in the Pennsylvania Railroad, we paid close attention to the barges that the company had built to transport coaches and freight cars across the Hudson River from New Jersey.

We soon had built our fleet of barges to make the crossing from Norfolk to the eastern shore of Virginia, due to convincing the railroad to completing the construction of the rail line to Cape Charles.

Our steamboats connected the western and eastern shores of Maryland, and now our rail lines reached down from Alexandria to Reedville where our Menhaden fleet was based. On the Eastern shore our rail lines now connected to Cambridge, Salisbury, Chestertown and Easton, all of which were booming towns with tobacco, corn, tomatoes and strawberries and all manner of seasonal produce such as watermelon keeping our skipjacks and trains running goods to the cities of Washington, Baltimore, Norfolk, Philadelphia and on to New York and Chicago.

CHESAPEAKE 1880

One town that connected three rail lines was the town of Ridgely, Maryland. Located in the center of fine bountiful land with a long growing season, the Pennsylvania had built a modest but attractive railway station. One Virginia entrepreneur had bought one hundred acres of land and was in the process of setting up a chicken farm along with raising soybeans, a new crop that some believed would have a good future.

The main north-south rail line dipped down from Wilmington; Delaware ran through Ridgely and down to Hurlock and points south on the way to Cape Charles where we had built a terminal for our rail barges.

As we needed various regulatory approvals from Virginia, keeping the good graces of Gov. Cameron was essential.

Since he really took a beating in the Norfolk papers for his great adventure with the oyster pirates, I thought I might send a note to my brother to request the assistance of the *Washington Herald*.

The economy of the Chesapeake Bay region depended greatly on produce, oysters, crabs, rockfish, menhaden and timber. Cutting, growing catching, peeling and shucking crops and seafood provided good jobs for many folks, especially the former slaves and their offspring.

The standard of living for Negroes in the region had been changing from living in shanties to better homes, depending mostly on the jobs they were able to obtain after the end of plantation life. Low ambition had a predictable outcome. But the old ways of some white folks meant that the education provided in schools wasn't going to be available for most Negroes. I had made a decision long ago in my business. Our company never had slave labor with wages always paid to Negroes based on their value of work, no difference for colored or white. That was the same standard applied to any deckhand, steward, engine room crew, master of a vessel or office workers.

Since our buyboats, steamboats, tugs, and now our rail business all paid wages for honest work, the standard of living for our employees was on the upper end of most towns in which they lived, including the Negroes who always lived in one section of the towns in the tidewater region.

Due to the history of our companies, we maintained good relations with our employees and began to find ways to be sure that their children were able to complete a solid secondary education as we moved towards the twentieth century.

Not all of our competitors operated the same way that Old Bay Line did, and strife with their workforce led to a great commotion from time to time.

One of our rail lines reached over to the Ocean east of Salisbury where I hoped to one day see a resort come to life. There were but a few rooming houses and cottages along the shore.

The construction of a rail line and bridge across Assawoman Bay moved forward and we would be counting on city folks taking the trains to the Maryland beach the same way they did to Atlantic City which had been connected to Philadelphia by rail in recent years.

Several Baltimore bankers believed in the plan and not only bought stock in our rail line but also bought sizeable tracts of scrub pine and sand dunes. Who knows if anything but wild ponies will ever be there?

One entrepreneur from Colorado appeared on the western shore and bought up land along the shoreline in Calvert County. Walter Mears was his name, and he convinced a few dozen investors to give him the money to build a rail line to the new town he called Chesapeake Beach.

When I received a note from him asking to meet at the Willard Hotel in Washington, I cordially responded that the requested date would be acceptable.

Our meeting took place on a bright fall day in the bustling restaurant that served heads of state, members of Congress and Presidents.

The marble floors, high ceilings and walls of black walnut accommodated the movers and shakers of the nation's capital city.

Impeccable service from capable waiters took our orders for supper and provided us with a delicious meal. Afterward, Mears suggested we retire to the men's bar for brandy and cigars.

"You might be wondering why I invited you to meet with me, Mr. Douglas," offered Mears.

"I had a pretty good idea what might be on your mind given the great achievement you have accomplished in building your railroad to Chesapeake Beach in under one year," I responded. "You not only dealt with the scalawags in government but you crossed several significant waterways with bridges as well."

"Mr. Douglas I believe we have mutual business interests," said Mears.

"Certainly sir, you don't need me to help you with a railroad, you have just built your own, not only in record time but with a resort destination that you also own. What else can be on your mind?"

"I would like you to build a steamship pier at my resort, a pier to which you would have the exclusive right to dock your steamers," answered Mears.

"Ha, I should have seen that coming," I answered. "But if you can build your railroad, why can't you build your pier?"

"Two reasons," said Mears. "One, is that I have never built any maritime structures such as a pier and the second is that the water is so shallow that the pier would have to be a mile long jutting out into the Chesapeake Bay. At this point all of the capital raised for my endeavors have been exhausted on building a rail line, buying locomotives and rolling stock, the coaches and luggage cars, the boardwalk and three hotels."

"Are you telling me that you are out of money and can't raise anymore?" I said with a bit of amazement.

"I believe that your steamship line would prosper with bringing travelers to Chesapeake Beach and become a popular stop on your scheduled services between Norfolk, Baltimore and Washington," said Mears ending his spiel with a flourish.

"Have you already approached my competitors with this offer," said I, suspecting that he had done so and been turned down, but wondering if he was honest enough to admit his plight.

"I have, but I found no taker. I hope you won't be irritated that I failed to bring the offer to you first, but I believed that since you are in the railroad business you might find investing in my Chesapeake Beach Railway Company to be risky, due to our unproven goals," replied Mears.

"I have to admit that I don't like being consulted far down on a list but since you are talking about something in the area of $10 a foot to build a decent pier, this is a lot of money to risk."

"Should you decide to join me in this endeavor, I am prepared to not only give Old Bay Line exclusive docking rights, since you essentially have built your own pier, but an opportunity to build a hotel of your own on land provided at no cost."

"Mr. Mears, I have to require that you provide more than that."

"Yes, Captain, what might that be?"

"I will need to have fifty-one percent ownership in the Casino and any racetrack that you build."

At that point Mears agreed; we had a glass of brandy to seal the deal and the next day Alan Cecil, my attorney in Washington, would draw up the papers. Now the Douglas family was expanding into gambling and racetracks, and I couldn't help but wonder what my grandfather, Capt. Douglas would have to say about dealing with such wickedness as card players.

We had seen many con-men and card sharks operate in the Grand Saloons of the ships over the years, sometimes being escorted down the gangplank by our crew. A few left in the middle of the night by unknown means after fleecing other passengers. Being a riverboat gambler had its risks and rewards.

Point of Rocks, Md. Baltimore and Ohio Railroad station at the junction of the Main Line and Metropolitan branch to Washington, D.C. This view looks west to Chicago.

CHAPTER TEN

Slavery to Captain

Life on Smith Creek in Maryland, located just north of Point Lookout was about as pleasant as could be for the Biscoe family.

Thelma and Ignatius Biscoe had been freed by their master a year before the 'War of Northern Aggression' as the Civil War was known in Maryland.

The state was held in the Union by force with the first bloodshed taking place when federal troops were fired on by a pro-South mob in Baltimore. The General Assembly had been blocked from seceding, but that didn't change the sympathies and sentiments of the region's population.

Thelma and Ignatius, who was known by most simply as "Nat", had raised seven children and were given 100 acres of land along the Chesapeake Bay and Smith Creek.

Capt. Smith owned the land that had been carved out from St. Michael's Manor. Smith – who then decided to carve up his original land-grant plantation and provide for each of his slaves, along with his family.

Thelma and Nat were among the twenty slave families that had been given land and timber to cut to build log cabins and build log boats. They were also given livestock to start their small farms.

In Nat's case, since he had been a crewmember of Capt. Smith's Buyboat, twenty years later he was also given Capt. Smith's buyboat – an unbelievable event. Nat and Thelma were stunned at the legal papers given to them by Capt. Smith and presented to them on July 4, 1880.

"Nat," said Capt. Smith the day he had turned over the legal title to the boat, "I am going to give you some advice."

"Yassir, I can use all the advice I can get, this very kind decision of yours to give me your boat along with a farm knocks me off my feet, Cap'n.," said Nat.

"You've been a loyal part of my family and business for forty years both as a slave and a tenant farmer and now as neighbor, Nat, and God willing, I will be around to help you should you need it. "

"This advice I'll give you without you asking: never join in with the oyster pirates, no matter what kind of offer they give you, that band of pirates will be robbing everyone on the Bay for generations.

"I 'spect I'd agree with dat," said Nat.

"I told Capt. Douglas what I am doing and he warned me that many of the captains will be resentful of a colored man owning his buyboat."

"Dat's true, Cap'n, they don't like me too much just as a crewman and sure don't like it too much that I have my farm. Not all of them, mind you, but a right smart bunch of them make no bones about how they feel."

"When you tie up on Saturday evening, just go home to your family just like you do today, never drink with the captains or play cards. Their favorite deal is to get a new owner of a boat drunk and have him lose his vessel in a crooked card game."

"Cap'n, I am not trying to pry into your business, but you gave away all of your plantation and now your boat?"

"I told you twenty years ago that there was a war coming, and I was worried that the days of slavery would end with much turmoil. Well, we lived through what happened to our country. Now life is better in many ways as we rebuild the tidewater region and the South. My only son is a lawyer in Washington, and I have given him my investments, and he makes a lot of money working for the Old Bay Line. That leads me to one other item of business between us."

"Yassir, Cap'n," said Nat.

"I am recommending that you associate your boat with the Old Bay Line as should you decide to fly the colors of Old Bay, you will have the protection of Capt. Douglas. I talked to him about this, and he agreed with one stipulation."

"I can figure what that might be as he is a hard bargain," said Nat.

"This is his hard bargain – he wants you to tell folks that inquire that you had to sign over fifty-one percent of your boat to his company."

"I was afraid of that."

"The rest of the deal is that you will retain legal title to one hundred percent but no one is to know about that part."

"Bye-de-Gawd, Cap'n, that is mighty fine of him to do that, I don't 'spect anyone will be too anxious to pull any tricks like cutting our lines in port and such if they think Cap'n Douglas owns the *Thelma B*."

Nat had renamed the buyboat after his wife Thelma after Capt. Smith gave it to him. She was delighted; the only colored woman in the Potomac area to have a boat named after her.

The lives of the Biscoe family had changed significantly since the war. There was talk of a new school for colored being built near St. Inigoes and one of their daughters – Sadie - had been accepted into the Sisters of Charity convent in Baltimore.

Their son Vincent had become first mate and learned the buyboat business from Nat was his passion. John, Dennis, and Bartholomew ran the farm and tonged for oysters in the winter. The two youngest girls, Martha, and Eloise, were still working on the farm and going to grade school in the winter.

Picking crabs is a hands-on task. Library of Congress

CHAPTER ELEVEN

Six lost during Storm

As reporters for the *Washington Herald*, my sons Jack and Allen often traveled on our steamers between Washington and Baltimore as well as Norfolk when major news stories demanded coverage.

On a trip on the *George Washington* past Taylors Island while working the Eastern Shore ports, a sudden thunderstorm crackled across the Chesapeake.

The *George Washington* was a large steamship and the newest in the fleet of the Old Bay Line.

Waves ran up to 20 feet and even though gear and cargo were lashed down, the pounding of the ship by the wind and sea began to take its toll.

Fifty barrels of North Carolina sweet potatoes had been loaded on the stern deck and lashed down but one by one the lines securing the barrels began to break, quickly sending the barrels of potatoes flying off the ship. The *George Washington* left a trail of barrels in its wake as the Captain managed to turn the ship into the Eastern Bay at Bloody Point.

Capt. Pepper Langley held on tight in the wheelhouse as the helmsman struggled to maintain control, fighting the wind. As the *George Washington* passed the buoy marker for the Miles River, the wind lessened. Still, though the waves were smaller, one after another crashed over the deck. The engine room crew struggled with the ship's pumps to keep the sea water from gaining in the bilges.

In another hour, the battered steamship was tying up at the wharf in St. Michaels.

Only as the ship tied up did the fate of six crewmen become known, as when it was time to secure the lines, they didn't respond to their posts. A search of the ship confirmed that six of the crew were gone in the storm.

Jack and Allen rushed to the telegraph office on the main street of town to file their story.

Six Feared Dead in Tragedy on Chesapeake

The Washington Herald

ST. MICHAELS, MD. – While sailing from Cambridge to Baltimore the Old Bay Liner George Washington was hit hard by a sudden summer thunderstorm in which six crewmen are believed to have perished.

The crewmen were attempting to prevent a cargo of sweet potatoes from being swept overboard when mooring lines securing them to the afterdeck broke as the ship pitched hard in twenty-foot waves.

More details and names of those lost overboard will be wired shortly.

Once again, Mother Nature had changed the course of the lives of those who work on the Chesapeake Bay.

Weather had come to claim its toll from man on the open seas of the Bay.

Capt. Langley and his first mate inspected the damage, made provisions for repairs and wired the main office of Old Bay Line in Baltimore with a report.

When checking to see which men had been lost in the storm, Capt. Langley realized one of those swept overboard was his grandson Kevin.

"Hire every boat in this port and send them out with torches to look for our men," said Capt. Langley.

***

The search went on till morning without success, and the boats returned empty-handed.

At about daylight, the bodies of the six crewmen of the *George Washington* were discovered on the sandy shore of Tilghman Island by a lad out to check his crab pots. Several dozen barrels of sweet potatoes also dotted the shoreline.

The boy's father had been one of those participating in the night-long search of the Eastern Bay. He sent the teen by horseback to St. Michael's with the sad news while he and a neighbor began to load the bodies into a wagon to take to town.

The Langley family had its share of tragedy, as did most families on the Bay during the war years. Weather, fires and sudden scourges of flu also took lives away from vibrant and flourishing clans when least expected.

The hardworking tidewater people of the Langley family took the turmoil in stride keeping their hope and faith alive on the water and in the pews of the bleached white wooden Methodist Church on Solomon's Island.

Kevin had been the only Solomon's crewman who had died in the storm, and his funeral stopped the *George Washington* for the day as his grandfather attended his funeral on the shore overlooking the blue Patuxent River.

The other five crewmen were all from the town of Crisfield, which held their funerals the following day. The notice of their names had gone out with an update from Jack and Allen with their news story to the Washington Herald via telegraph and relayed around the Bay. The harbor filled with the workboats and steamships bringing hundreds of persons to pay their respects to the five families of Crisfield.

Crisfield had become a center of the seafood industry with a bustling collection of shucking houses, processing plants and dozens of buyboats and workboats plying the harbor each day. A rail line had been built to move the vast quantities of crabs, fish, and oysters to markets. The rail line stopped at the small

Marion Station on the way to connect with the mail line between Norfolk and Wilmington.

The tragedy hit the Old Bay Line family hard as all six of those lost had many relatives who worked in various segments of my business, on the water, on the rails and in the seafood plants.

Of the six men lost, four of them had families of their own with a total of fourteen children left without fathers.

Capt. Cullison had started a watermen's fund before I bought his fleet of buyboats and as we both invested in railroads and added more steamships we put a portion of profits into the fund each year.

This tragedy was the first time in ten years we had suffered the loss of an employee. At least we could assure the widow that her husband's paycheck would continue. A small consolation to be sure, but I believed it the right thing to do when considering the risk of being on a ship. The Watermen's Fund was invested in railroad stocks and commercial properties in Washington and had done well, leaving the financial future of those devastated families on an even keel.

CHESAPEAKE 1880

Tongers selling oysters to a buyboat.

CHAPTER TWELVE
The Sweet Potatoes and Tipsy Tug Captain

In the Manokin River just off of Tangier Sound in Somerset County, Maryland, was a master carpenter – Frank Laird. One of the finest around, he built sturdy vessels to work the Bay. One of the nine-log sailing bugeyes he built was the *Wm. B. Tennison.* With a shallow draft, the sixty foot bugeye was ideal for dredging for oysters. Two brothers, Russell and Benjamin Miles of Monie, Maryland had ordered the *Tennison* from Laird became the first owners of a vessel that would lead a long life.

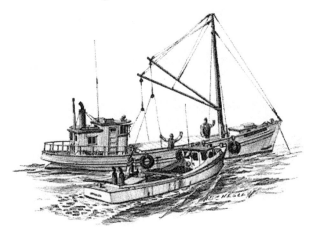

"William B. Tennison" buying oysters

Wm. B. Tennison is buying oysters. Calvert Marine Museum

Solid logs long enough to build such a craft were becoming scarce, and the shipyards of the Bay were soon manufacturing the cheaper and easier to operate skipjacks.

The *Tennison* was able to show a nice profit for the Miles brothers who would haul produce and timber in the summer and oysters in the winter. Summer months would find the *Tennison* loaded with produce from Albemarle Sound in North Carolina and as far north as Port Deposit.

The Tennison was converted to power in 1908 and was used as a buyboat during the oyster season by her new owners. In 1910, the Tennison had been purchased by Alphonse Hazelwood of Eclipse, Virginia.

The *Tennison* had three bunks and galley with a table for eating.

One of the crews of any oyster dredger or buyboat was always chosen to be the cook due to superior abilities at preparing the good food necessary for providing the strength needed to work eighteen-hour days.

Capt. Hazelwood had a recipe for oyster stew he prepared himself on the *Tennison.* It was easy to make and during the oyster season, the stew was always on the galley stove.

Simple to fix, with bacon fried in an iron skillet; onions and celery added to the bacon along with rosemary, black pepper and thyme and then a gallon of oysters. After cooking the oysters thoroughly, the entire large skillet contents were put into a stock pot with a gallon of milk and half pound of butter. On occasion, even potatoes or carrots were added.

This hardy stew was acceptable for any meal of the day accompanied by biscuits or cornbread.

The tough life of a buyboat captain didn't end with storms and pirates. Other captains were sometimes a problem, especially if they were drunk.

This story appeared in the *Washington Herald*:

Harbor Collision Upsets the Taters

Norfolk, Va. --- The tugboat *Mabel* collided with a bay freighter this past evening resulting in the loss of some cargo and damage to the freighter.

The *Wm. B. Tennison* steamed north towards Norfolk with a load of sweet potatoes from Elizabeth City, N.C., late yesterday, expecting to arrive about nine pm, hoping to unload and continue on to Baltimore and arrive there by dawn.

As the bay freighter approached the steamboat dock in Norfolk, *Mabel*, a tugboat, suddenly roared in the path of the *Tennison* from behind a large steamship. The tug smashed into the *Tennison,* which was loaded down with 500 barrels of sweet potatoes.

Capt. Al Hazelwood reports his vessel suffered damage of about $500 and the loss of 210 barrels of potatoes.

The *Mabel* is a Norfolk & Western Railroad tug used to push train cars across the Chesapeake. No damage was reported to the tug, but the inebriated captain of the tug is expected to stand the loss of his master's license due to being drunk.

Kecoughtan ties up at Virginia landing.

A Buyboat dealing with oystermen at Rock Point on the Wicomico in Charles County, Md.

Steamer *Chesapeake*

CHAPTER THIRTEEN

Competition

Old Bay Line continued to have tough competition on the Washington D.C. runs though it was dominant in the middle and upper Bay.

My four main competitors were the Inland and Seaboard Coasting Company, the Clyde Line, Washington Steamship Company Ltd. And the Potomac Steamboat Company. My brother William's line, the Norfolk, and Baltimore Company was larger than Old Bay and for good reason – it was Williams sole project and he grew it well.

The Inland and Seaboard ran the *John Gibson* and *E. C. Knight* on the New York run. The *Knight* was lost in a collision with a schooner near Hog Island and the following year the New York run was simply abandoned and the *Gibson* sold in 1884.

The older vessels of the Inland and Seaboard, the *Lady of the Lake* and the *Jane Mosely* were still on the

124

run to Norfolk from Washington until 1892. With a heavy investment into palatial steamers by the Norfolk and Washington Steamboat Company, those vessels were soon unable to compete and sought routes where they could do business. The *John W. Thompson* was the flagship of Inland and Seaboard Coasting until the line was closed, and then the ship was sold to E. S. Randall and renamed the *Harry Randall*.

The Old Bay Line began to see serious completion by 1900 as some lines consolidated and others went out of business. The Clyde Line had begun operations with the side-wheeler *Sue* in 1878 and stopped at all the river landings between Washington and Baltimore. The *Sue* was soon purchased by Charles Lewis, who owned the *John E. Taggart* and then sold out the bustling Weems Line.

The Weems Line was out to be the principal competition with Old Bay Line. With its new *Northumberland* placed into service, replacing its iron screw *Potomac*, and adding the *Anne Arundel* and then the *Three Rivers*, each upgrade meant more competition for the passenger trade and larger cargo holds to pick up the freight business.

By 1906, the Chesapeake and Potomac Steamboat Company had acquired the Randall Line and changed the name of the *Harry Randall* to the *Capital City*.

George E. Mattingly was a shrewd operator of steamships and owned the Potomac Steamboat Company. His ships, the *Excelsior* and *George Leary* and his line were taken over by the Norfolk and Washington Steamboat Company in 1891. The *Excelsior* had been built for the purpose of moving railroad cars across Aquia Creek for the connection between Richmond and Washington. Picking up passengers from Washington to

Quantico until the railroad bridges were completed was an important part of their business.

As the turn of the century approached, the competition for Old Bay Line had grown to new levels, making it tough to see the profits as in earlier years.

The Norfolk and Washington Steamboat Company began operations in 1891 the screw steamers *Washington* and *Norfolk* were like floating palaces. In 1895, the company inaugurated the even larger *Newport News*; in 1905 the *Southland* and in 1912 the *Northland* entered service on the Chesapeake. Smaller lines ran smaller ships to smaller venues such as the flat-bottomed *Mary Washington,* which ran an excursion route to White House and Occoquan from 1873 to 1882. The *McAlester* joined the *Pilot Boy* in runs from Washington to Mount Vernon and Marshall Hall. The *River Queen* had carried President Lincoln to visit the Union Army at Petersburg during the Civil War, and 30 years was still plying the Potomac taking colored passengers from Washington to Notley Hall and Glymont.

Colonial Beach on the Virginia shore of the Potomac was established as a resort and just before 1900 was the destination of intensive excursion traffic from the city on ships such as *T.V. Arrowsmith*, the *Jane Mosely, Harry Randall and St. Johns.*

Grand foyer of Norfolk & Western steamship. *Francis Benjamin Johnson photo Library of Congress*

The Steamer *Majestic*, Boston, Mass. LoC.

CHAPTER FOURTEEN

The Crab-Catchers

Among the popular stops along the Potomac was Tolson's Pier at Piney Point. The landing boasted a fine pier and comfortable hotel. A swimming beach in front of the hotel and the nearby lighthouse and keeper's house that had often been a summer retreat for Presidents prior to the Civil War.

Interior of a Chesapeake Bay steamship.

One fine July day before the turn of the century a family arrived on the *George Washington* for a month-long stay at Tolson's Hotel. The family had been traveling to Piney Point for several years along with a grandmother and a dog. With two boys and a daughter, this summer resort was something the family looked forward to the entire school year. The youngest boy was a lad named Charlie, all of ten years old and already an expert at snagging plump soft-shell crabs. Charlie netted the soft-shell crabs from the grasses along the edges of the creeks back along the coves leading inland from the river. Using a skiff and a crab net, the now experienced crab-catcher Charlie was able to provide his family with the great tasting soft crabs for dinner but picked up some pocket change by selling several dozen soft crabs each to the Tolson's and the nearby Swann's Pier.

Charlie had been up at dawn that day and walked down the lane the nearby creek on the far side of the field behind the hotel where he untied the skiff his father had rented for him for a month.

With his crab-net already in the 15' wooden skiff built from white pine, Charlie was off for another great adventure. His older brother Brooks had been his crabbing companion in previous summers but this year had picked up a job as a mate on a charter fishing boat making the unheard-of sum of one dollar each day. Since the vacationers were drinking a bit while fishing, at times, he was given tips as well as his pay from the boat captain.

A draketail crabbing boat decked out with crabbing gear.

Charlie rounded the mouth of the inlet and ducked into another small creek with a narrow mouth. On the shore of the creek were two colored boys who were netting crabs as they were pulled into the creek with the current. Charlie paddled up to the shore in his skiff and beached it so he could watch this great way to catch crabs. In less than a half hour the two boys, both about the same age as

Charlie had caught a full bushel of crabs and loaded it into a nearby wagon. They got another bushel basket out of their wagon and began to fill it as well.

When one particularly jumbo crab swam by, the shorter boy reached out to snag it and lost his footing, quickly sinking into the water over his head. He bobbed up and gasped for air and screamed as his brother stood on the shore and wailed for help, screaming towards Charlie that neither he nor his brother could swim.

Charlie had learned to swim at the age of four and quickly jumped into the creek and swam over to the last spot he had seen the boy go under the surface. He dove down, grabbed him by the shirt and dragged him to shore where he pushed on his back and raised his arms as he had been shown to assist a drowned person.

The young boy coughed and sputtered. Soon he was breathing fine, and his brother stopped crying.

"You saved my brother's life," said Moses. "We owe you, what is your name?"

"Charlie, glad to help you but how come you guys can't swim?" said Charlie.

"We in the country don't bother with learning how to swim if we just take care not to go in over our heads, but my brother Tom got a little greedy goin' after that big-in'." answered Moses.

"Well, if you can teach me how to catch crabs by the bushel, I'll teach you both how to swim," said Charlie.

"What will we do with so many crabs," asked Moses.

"Heck, I've been selling my soft-crabs to the cooks at the hotels, but since last week I've also been selling to the cooks on the steamboats that stop here every day, aren't you doing the same thing?"

"No, we take them to the hotels, one here on Piney Point, and then we cross the channel to St. George Island sell them to that hotel too but if we can sell them to the steamboats. I'll bet we could catch plenty mo' crabs," answered Moses, calculating in his mind and counting on his fingers on what he hoped they might make.

Within a week, both Moses and his nearly-drowned brother Abraham had learned to swim and the new team of crab-catchers had begun to sell crabs by the bushel to each steamboat that stopped everyday, at least twice a day.

Word of Charlie saving the life of Abraham got back to the hotel. The owner refunded the cost of the boat rental to his dad in appreciation of his heroism. Abraham's grandfather, Nat Biscoe, appeared at the hotel and brought a cured ham for Charlie's family to take back to Alexandria where they lived - as a thank you for the family.

Charlie thought nothing of saving Abraham and counted his blessings at being there to meet such champion crab-catchers.

The grandfather of Moses and Abraham had another surprise.

Nat Biscoe pulled into Tolson's Pier on his newest buyboat, *Captain Jim,* just ahead of the *Northland*, which was about two miles off in the distance.

The three boys sat on the pier with their wagon piled high with six bushels of crabs.

"Grandpa, we have never seen you stop in here before," said Moses.

"You're right boy, at this time of day we are usually on our way to Crisfield, but today we decided to stop and find out of you have any crabs to sell," said Nat.

"We sure do," answered the three boys in chorus.

"How much do the ships pay you for your crabs?"

"We get anywhere from fifty cents to perhaps seventy-five cents," answered Moses.

'Well, today only, I am in the market for some big fat crabs, can I buy all six bushels on your wagon?"

"Sure," answered the boys at the same time.

"Are you sure the *Northland* won't be disappointed?"

"Don't care if they are as that fancy ship is the hardest one to make any money off of, last week they would only pay us a quarter a bushel," said Moses.

"Well I have some special customers and I'll make you a deal, if you promise to save the money I pay you, keeping but a dollar for each of you to spend, I am going to pay you five dollars for each bushel."

"It's a deal ," Moses said with immediate agreement from his brother and Charlie.

The boys beamed as the transaction was completed, and Nat Biscoe's buyboat pulled away from the pier with its load of expensive crabs.

When Charlie's family headed back to the city at the end of the month both Charlie and his brother, Brooks had picked up plenty of money to save for new bikes. The family had a fine country ham for the Christmas holidays, and Charlie had new friends and business to return to the following summer.

***

On the way back to Alexandria on the *CAPTAIN DOUGLAS*, Charlie and his family listened intently to the

News Reader bring the passengers up to date on the latest news.

"Greetings everyone and thank you for traveling with the Old Bay Line," said Jack Douglas. "We have a number items from the front page of a recent edition of *The Bee* of Washington, D.C."

THE BEE, Washington, D.C.

Home Rule, Industry, Justice, Equality, and Recognition according to Merit

JUSTH'S OLD STAND,

LADIES' AND GENTLEMEN'S
First-Class Second-Hand Clothing,
BOOTS, SHOES, HATS. ETC.
619 D. St. Bet. 6th and 7th Sts. N. W.

Real Estate & Loans Negotiated
Reliable persons can obtain small sums of money by applying to
W. Augustus Stewart
Office room corner of 10tb and F street
Residence, 1703 19th street. N. W.
All notices attended to promptly.

HOUSE AND WALL PAINTING, GRAINING, &C.

J. T. STEWART,

Orders left at the office of The Bee will be promptly attended to. 1107 IStreet, N. W.

Levi McCabe Caterer.

Meals Served Out,

Table Board.

922 11th Street, N. W.

W. H. Harrover

Manufacturer of

STOVES. RANGES AND FURNACES,

And dealer in Table Cutlery, Tinware, House
Furnishings Goods, etc., 313 Seventh Street,
Northwest and Pennsylvania Avenue,
Washington, D.C.

Philadelphia House,

WILLIAMS & MEREDITH,

Proprietors.

348 Penn, Avenue, N. W.

E. MURRAY,

Ice Cream Parlors,

1118 K STREET.

First-class Cream Wholesale and Retail.

Orders promptly attended to.

REST not. Life is sweeping by, go and dare before you
die. Something mighty and Sublime leave behind to
conquer time, $96 a week in your town- $5 out risk-
134

free. No risk. Everything new; Capital is not required. We will furnish you everything. Many are making fortunes. Ladies make as much as men, and boys and girls make great pay. Reader, if you want a business at which you can make great pay all the time write for particulars to Hallet & Co. Augusta, Maine

M. KETSKEMETHY,

Photographer, 1109 Penn. Avenue, Washington, D. C. First class carbine, photos $3.00 per dozen, card photos, $2.00 per dozen.

NOTICE. To every dozen pictures one extra is added finished in fine watercolors. In a half dozen, one out of the six finished in fine watercolors. It is the only place in the city where yon can get this benefit.

GO TO CHASE'S

Ice Cream Saloon

And Confectionery Resort!

Foreign and Domestic Fruits, Ginger Ale, Soda, French Cakes, Pies, Biscuits, Rolls, every day, Alderney Milk.

OYSTERS FRIED & STEWED

Cigars and Tobacco. 119 I Street, N. W.

LATEST NEWS.

SHIPPING ON FIRE

Burning of a Dock and Vessels – A number of persons injured

NEW YORK: A spark from an engine fell into a pile of jute that had just been landed on Harbeck's dock, Brooklyn, from the ship *Lawrence E Delap* from Calcutta. The dock was filled with hemp, jute, and coffee. The flames spread with incredible rapidity, and in a few minutes the entire dock was ablaze.

The *Delap* was the first vessel to catch fire, and all her rigging was burnt before she could be towed out. Next to her on the south side of the dock was the ship *Perseverance*, also from Calcutta, and on the north side lay the ship *Col. Adams*, from Calcutta.

To both of these vessels the flames wore communicated, and the crews jumped overboard for safety. When the firemen reached the dock, the supports of the roof gave way and the roof fell in, burying over a dozen firemen and dock hands beneath the ruins. A rescuing party was quickly formed, and the men were dragged out from the blazing rafters. None was killed outright, but all were more or less burned and bruised. Firemen, McNamara, McDonald, and McDougall, of hook and ladder truck No. 3, were injured seriously about the body. The loss on the vessels and cargoes will amount to over $500,000.

Panic in Egypt Over Cholera

London, July 19. The panic in Alexandria Egypt, over the appearance of the cholera, is increasing. The number of deaths from the disease in Cairo, Wednesday was 68.

The Empress Augusta, of Germany, is suffering from partial paralysis.

It is believed that the differences between France and England are in the process of amicable adjustment.

A number of French financial houses have offered M. de Lesseps all the money required to construct a new canal or to widen the present one.

Sir Charles Michael Wolseley, the baronet, was married yesterday to Miss Anita Theresa Murphy, the daughter of Mr. D. T. Murphy, of San Francisco.

The secretary of the English consul at Tamatave has been liberated, the captain of the English gunboat Dryad assuming all responsibility for him

Mr. Charles Bradlaugh has brought an injunction against the sergeant-at-arms of the House of Commons to prevent him from keeping Mr. Bradlaugh from his seat.

The cotton caterpillar has appeared in the section of Selma, Ala. An examination of the crop near the city shows that the top leaves are badly riddled. Plenty of worms are in sight and webbed up. The crop is three weeks late, and the worms are in such numbers and have appeared so early that the prospects for the crop are gloomy.

The conference committee on the Pennsylvania Legislative and Senatorial Appointment bill reported their inability to agree.

An effort was made to have other committees appointed, but, without action, the Senate adjourned until Monday evening, after adopting a resolution for final adjournment on the 24th inst. No business was transacted in the House. There is now but little prospect of an agreement upon the apportionment legislation, for which the extra session was called.

The Mexican consul at Tucson, Arizona, has received a letter from the frontier, under date of July 14, stating that near the place where Gen. Crook left the hostiles, in the district of Montezuma, they attacked a Mexican settlement and killed five persons.

KEN ROSSIGNOL

The New Orleans Board of Health has adopted a resolution advising the Governor to issue a proclamation establishing quarantine against all Mexican, South American, and West India ports, to take effect immediately.

Swainmau, who was arrested at Nashville, Tenn., for stealing the ledger that is so important in the Polk trial, has confessed that he took it at the instigation of ex-Treasurer Polk, and that he received $175 for doing it.

Not since the day that President Garfield was shot has so much excitement been witnessed in this city as was caused by the report that Gen. Grant had dropped dead in New York. It is believed it was used as a signal for the telegraph operators to stop work, and at that moment all the telegraphers belonging to the brotherhood left their desks. The strike was general throughout the United States and Canada.

A telegram was received at the Department of State to-day from Mr. Campbell, United States consul at Monterey, dated at Laredo, Texas, confirming the press report of the assault upon Mr. Shaw while acting as consul at Monterey.

The strike of the telegraphers began the 19th inst., all over the country. Fifteen thousand members of the Brotherhood quit work. In Baltimore, 112 operators left their desks, and business was seriously impeded there as elsewhere.

GENERAL NEWS.

London, July 18. For the twenty-four hours ending at 8 A. M. yesterday, the deaths from cholera at Cairo were sixty-one. General Sir Evelyn Wood, who was about to leave for England, has been recalled by the Khedive on account of the existence of cholera in Cairo.

The American consul at Laredo, Mexico, has been mobbed, and papers and furniture destroyed.

It is now certain that the boy who testified at Nyiregyhaza, Hungary that he saw Jews kill a young girl committed perjury.

At a special meeting yesterday of the London Chamber of Commerce a resolution was adopted declaring that the question of the construction of a parallel Suez Canal should be referred to a royal commission.

There was a slight frost at Davenport, Iowa, on the 13th inst., but it did no damage.

Hanton won an easy sculling race at Ogdensburg, N. Y., over Ross. Hanton won by a quarter of a mile.

A Cuban political club, the object of which is to work for the independence of Cuba, has been organized in Philadelphia.

An express train was thrown from the track by a misplaced switch near Knoxville, Tenn., yesterday. The engine ran into the main building of the zinc works at that point, tearing away the whole side of the building.

John L. Heckmer, formerly mayor of Grafton, W. Va. and ex-supreme treasurer of the Catholic Knights of America, has made an assignment. He was interested in the furniture firm of Fronheise & Co., of Cumberland, Md.

A verdict for $5,475 has been given John Studebaker & Co., at Fort Wayne, Ind., against the United States Express Company. A package of $5,000 sent to plaintiff by express was found to contain only blank paper when opened at Fort Wayne.

London, July 17. --- A case believed to be cholera was discovered in Alexandria yesterday. The sanitary commission refuses to isolate the city. The disease is spreading throughout Egypt.

- Count de Chambord is improving.
- All of the French reinforcements have arrived at Tonquin.
- Sir Augustus Paget has been appointed British ambassador at Vienna.
- Articles of incorporation of the Delmonico Company, having for its object the building and leasing of hotels in the United States, were filed in New York.
- At Shenandoah, Pa., four stores on Upper Main street; were burned out: loss, $25,000: insurance, $10, 000,
  At Oxford, Ala., property of the value of $10,000: partially insured have burned out.
- Capt. J. D. Douglas, of the British bark *Erne*, has been arrested at Boston for violating the provisions of the new Chinese law in bringing from Manila a Chinaman whom he discharged and allowed to go ashore.
- A terrific furnace explosion occurred at Kutztown. Pa., in the anthracite furnace of the Philadelphia and Reading Railroad, eight boilers exploded, reducing the furnace to a mass of ruins. Frank Waltman was instantly killed; Solomon Waltman, his father, was badly injured; Henry Waltman was fatally injured; Morris Good was severely scalded: Engineer Marstella was badly injured, and a number of other employees slightly hurt.

- M. Waddington has been appointed ambassador of France to England.
- The American team yesterday competed for the cup and L5o presented to be shot for. The prize was won by Joiner.
- M. de Lesseps declares that a loan for building a second Suez Canal can be raised in France and other countries if England refuses to advance the money.
- The jury was sworn in the Polk trial at Nashville, Tenn. James C. Fleming, Polk's former clerk testified that in April, 1882, when the investigating committee was appointed to examine Polk's accounts, in order to meet a deficit resulting from a defalcation of $200,000 Polk deposited a number of fictitious drafts on various State depositories to make good the amount. When the examination was over, he withdrew these drafts.
- London, July 16 The French minister of foreign affairs said yesterday in the Chamber of Deputies that unexplained events in Madagascar could not impair the friendly relations of France and England.
- The cholera is spreading in Egypt.
- Officers have been arrested in Spain charged with plotting.
- A puree has been subscribed at Wimbledon to be sought for by the American riflemen there.
- The conservative members of Parliament have determined to oppose the new Suez Canal scheme. The British directors of the company have issued a report.

- The steamer *Beauhamois,* of Montreal with a pleasure party of 4,300 persons on board, ran upon a reef in the river Sunday and had to be run ashore, where she sank in eight feet of water. All of the excursionists were safely landed.
- An Act of the legislature of West Virginia, passed in 1877, makes the silver coins, issued by the United States a legal tender in that state for all debts, public and private. The trade dollar is one of these coins and is, therefore, a legal tender at their nominal value in West Virginia.
- The army-worm has made its appearance in the northern section of Lancaster County, Pa., in large numbers, and is committing ravages in the tobacco fields.
- It is reported from Havana that the American bark *Jose E. Moore*, Captain Carlisle that sailed from New York, June 23, for Sagua, will be sold for violation of customs laws.
- Fruit inspectors in New York have seized 30,000 watermelons brought from the South by the Savannah Steamship Company. They claim that the melons were rotten and unfit for use.
- National Transit Company has completed its oil pipeline to Baltimore.
- London is seriously alarmed about the cholera, which, it is stated by the cable, has made its appearance in that city.
- Ten new cases of small-pox were reported to the health commissioner at Lancaster,

Pa. Most of the new cases are of a mild type.

- A startling rumor reached Newport, R. I., to the effect that the steamer Lottie E. Merrill, of Tiverton, R. I. was lost off George's Banks, with all on board.
- Terrific storms are reported to be raging in the northwest. Hail, rain and wind have done incalculable damage to all classes of property and many lives are reported sacrificed.

London, July 15 --- A French officer boarded an English vessel at Tamatave recently and would allow the cargo to be landed only on the payment of duty. A sentry was placed on board the steamer.

Fire at Liptoszentimiklo, Hungary, has caused considerable loss of life. Twenty persons, including the prefect of police, are missing.

There was a riot at Roubaix, France, yesterday, in which the police commissioner was seriously injured. Six of the rioters were arrested.

It was rumored yesterday that Mr. Childers, English Chancellor of the Exchequer, would resign if the Suez Canal agreement were abandoned.

Cholera has appeared at Ghizeh, a suburb of Cairo, where there have been five deaths from the disease. A cordon has been established around the town.

A dispatch to the *London Standard* from Shanghai says that Japan has declined the proposal of M. Tricon, the French ambassador at Shanghai, to form an alliance against China.

The executive board of the Brotherhood of Telegraphers of the United States and Canada have presented to the officials of the Western Union Company in New York an increase in salaries, the abolition of compulsory Sunday work, and equal pay for both sexes.

The missing Tennessee ledger, in which the balances of state depositors were kept, which was stolen from the State Treasurers office last week, was found on the steps of Auditor's Office, was found to be intact, without mutilation or erasures in any part. Roland O. Swayne, formerly deputy clerk of the Supreme Court, was arrested at Nashville last evening on a warrant sworn out by State Treasurer Thomas, charging him with having abstracted the balance ledger from the treasurer's office.

The American horse 'Idea' has won the sweepstakes and one thousand crowns at Copenhagen.

J. Dreyfus, of the *France*, has been wounded in a duel with M. Judet, of the *Lanterne*.

The London Lancet says there is nothing in the Queen's condition to excite the slightest anxiety.

It is reported that the Czar has placed the Grand Duke Nicholas Constantinovitch under arrest for interfering in the government of Turkestan.

A slight shock of earthquake was felt at Cairo, Ill., Saturday morning.

"Filled" twenty-dollar gold pieces have appeared in Tennessee and other parts of the South.

Chas. Heywood Stratton, better known to the public as Gen. Tom Thumb, died at his residence at Marlboro, Mass., of apoplexy.

Reports from Sonora, Mexico, indicate that the Apaches are on the warpath.

Twelve persons are said to have been murdered near Oposura.

Elizabeth Stewart, the wife of a Reading (Pa.) minister, has been arrested Saturday, charged with cruelly beating a little girl named Rosa Strauss, who was in her employ.

The New Haven Wire Works, at East Haven, Conn., have been partly destroyed by fire. Loss about $30,000; fully insured. Three hundred men are temporarily thrown out of work.

Dr. John A. Warder, of North Bend, Ohio, is dead. He was a prominent member of the American forestry congress and the author of several works on fruit growing and tree culture.

Since October 1st the sale of leaf tobacco in the Lynchburg (Va.) warehouses have aggregated 16,733,670 pounds, an increase of 3,464,441 pounds compared with same months the previous year.

Twenty-five hundred pounds of powder exploded in the press-room in the upper yard of DuPont's powder works at Wilmington, Del. Thomas Pearl, foreman of the press-room, and Patrick Haley, a laborer, were killed, and Alexander Billingsby, another laborer, was slightly injured. Pearl had been employed at the works for twenty years. The building was damaged to the extent of $5,000.

The trial of Barbara Miller, colored, for the murder of her husband, Daniel Miller, in the Henrico County Court, Va., resulted in a verdict of being an accessory before the fact of murder in the first degree. She was sentenced to be hanged on September 14.

At New Lots, N. Y., during the thundershower, a black cloud over the eastern part of the village seemed to open suddenly, and a huge ball of fire shot through the air with a terrific report. Every house in the town was shaken. The bolt struck a tree at Vermont and Fulton Avenues and tore it to pieces. The ground around it was plowed up, and portions of the tree were found, fifty feet away.

KEN ROSSIGNOL

A hastily summoned Cabinet meeting was held in Mr. Gladstone's room in the House of Commons yesterday afternoon. It is believed it was in reference to the Madagascar affair.

Advices from Valparaiso state that there has been a heavy fall of snow in the Cordilleras. Two miles of the Transandine Telegraph Company's wires have been covered with snow for the last four days.

ROBINSON'S RESTAURANT

SPRING IS HERE AND SO AM I

AT

1226 Pa. Avenue, N. W.,

The BEST place for a good Meal and

Lunch in the City. Meals, 25 cents;

Lunches, 10, 15 and 20 cents.

MEAL TICKETS.

23 regular meal tickets for $5, ten twenty cent tickets for $1.90, ten fifteen cent tickets for $1.50, five 25 cent tickets for $1.15.

We have every convenience for sending Meals out to Ladies and gentlemen, also families. Breakfast from 7 to 10 A. M., dinner from 12 to 6 P.M.

Open from 6 A. M. to 12 P. M.

Furnished or unfurnished rooms with board by the day, week or month

Pension Clerks will find this the most convenient place in the city. We can serve you a first-class meal in ten minutes.

WANTED

100 TABLE BOABDEBS

AT ONCE

--- A Choice Assortment of ---

Fine Cigars, Cigarettes

AND TOBACCO

ALWAYS ON HAND

Having had many years of experience in catering we are now prepared to give entire satisfaction to all who will give us their patronage.

Don't forget name and number, 1226 Penn: Ave, Washington, D.C.

Interior view of a steamship

Maine Avenue waterfront of Washington, D.C.

Grand dining area of a steamship.

CHAPTER FIFTEEN

THE NEWS READERS

Jack and Allen had started reading the news to passengers on the steamboats on the runs between the Bay ports and Washington when they were but teens. Not only was the entertainment enjoyable for the guests but the boys accomplished a great deal of their education by gleaning the rapidly industrialization progress of the young nation from the ink on the pages they read.

Now, both near thirty and raising their families, made their travel time pass quickly by filling in at their former posts as 'news readers' on the steamships.

Allen was the reader on the *George Washington* when he took up a copy the *Norfolk Virginian* from April 9, 1895. The nation was changing in many ways with railroads successfully reuniting the torn nation after the War Between the States. Certainly, my fortunes had changed as well as I heeded the advice of Capt. Cullison to buy stock in railroads.

I sat back and listened as my son read the news with all the decorum of an actor to an audience that listened with great interest.

***

"Now Ladies and Gentlemen, lend me an ear!" announced Allen. "Our first article today is about the second invasion of the Yankees! Instead of pulling cannon and marching into our land with bayonets, they now are opening factories!"'

"This Norfolk newspaper has the following article on the topic:"

New England's Investigating Committee's Work Well Done.

As Businessmen, They are Slow to Discuss Results but are Decidedly Impressed with Southern Advantages and the Class of Mill Labor.

By Southern Associated Press

Raleigh, N. C., April 8, 1895 - The New England party of mill-owners reached Raleigh on a special train Sunday night. Mr. Ashley, president of the Chamber of Commerce, had gone down on the Raleigh and Augusta train to meet them and welcome them to our city. The party is composed of the most prominent mill owners in Massachusetts, one of whom owns 83,000,000 stock in New England cotton mills.

A number of prominent citizens called to see them in a special train. President Hoffman of the Seaboard Air-Line and Mr. D. A. Tompkins of Charlotte accompanied them.

The Eastern manufacturers during the day conversed about the handsome and profitable mills that they had seen

In the Carolinas and Georgia, and by the time they return to Massachusetts, they will be in possession of a fund of very valuable information regarding the industrial situation in the South. Mr. Lovering, president of the Arkwright Club and the Taunton Mills, said that it was, likely that the only use that would be made of the valuable information that had been obtained would be to present them to the Arkwright Club, which was a clothing organization, but it was likely that something would get out about the report.

While the committee does not indicate when or where a large cotton mill will be located as a result of the investigation, mill men who accompanied the party say that it would not be good business tact to comment on such matters.

They did say that they are strongly satisfied that the careful and systematic inquiry that is being made will result in the building in of at least one large mill in which New England capital will be largely interested.

The committee has expressed itself as being particularly struck with the favorable conditions of the factory labor, and were delighted to know that there was so much available labor which seems to be so well satisfied with its work. The investigations of the committee extend from the percentage of wastage to the rate of taxes, the number of the yarn to the profit per yard and every other question of detail.

The committee is taking a special interest in the water powers, but all along the line the trend of the investigations has been more on the line of the labor situation than anything else. The cost of coal has been found to be satisfactory, the supply of cotton entirely so and the welcome of the people most encouraging. The party finished its trip through the Piedmont section and left the South for home by the Bay Line steamship.

***

Instead of becoming bored of this news, many applauded as the contribution of capital to building factories and providing jobs was desperately needed in the South. I took particular note that the group of touring investors had availed themselves of transportation on both railroads and steamships in which I had significant investments.

***

"And now folks, we turn to an update on the weather!" said Allen.

"This is also from the *Norfolk Virginian*.

LOCAL WATER SPOUTS
Small Floods in Western Virginia – Damage to Property

By Southern Associated Press

LYNCHBURG, VA. April 8 – A special from Wytheville, Va. To the News says: The citizens of Wytheville awakened this morning to find the heavy rains during the night had created a flood in the streams, rivalling the famous flood of 1878; the difference being that this flood, they lacking two or three feet of being as high, the river rose much more rapidly and did equally as much damage. Fences, logs, bridges, lumber and livestock were caught by the swelling streams and carried down with irresistible force. The railroad track in the neighborhood of Max Meadows was flooded, and there have been no trains from either direction today.

Dr. S. R Sayers had a hundred sheep, and two colts drowned. The streams are reported so high that a number of other casualties are expected and that news is cut off from the greater part of the county. So far as can be learned the rain was continued to Southwest Virginia but was so heavy in places as to indicate local weather spouts.

The flood is receding very rapidly and by morning the streams will be within their banks.

LYNCHBURG SHUT OUT!

The strong Pittsburg team played the Lynchburg's today, and the local team was shut out, the first time this season. The Smoky City sluggers hit the ball hard and often and when the game closed they had twenty runs to their credit. The Lynchburgers hit the ball very well, but they were too scattered to net any runs. Score: Pittsburg 20 – Lynchburg 0.

Resuming Work

By Southern Associated Press

PITTSBURG, PA. April 8. – Fifty miners, protected by the same number of Deputy Sheriff's resumed work at Mauoun, on the Monongahela River this morning. The Jumbo mine of Robbins & Company at McDonald, also started this morning with fifteen men guarded with deputies. The strikers will attempt to have the new men quit work, and if they refuse trouble is feared at both places. The operators held a meeting this afternoon for the purpose of discussing the strike situation.

***

Allen sensed that his audience might be getting drowsy and suddenly bolted up onto a chair, balancing himself as the ship slowly rocked with the choppy Potomac.

***

"And now a news flash from Florida," said Allen with his voice raised.

IN THE HANDS OF RECEIVERS

PENSACOLA, FLORIDA – The Southern States Land and Timber Company, one of the largest concerns doing business here, was placed in the hands of three receivers today by order of Judge Pardo, of New Orleans. This firm is an English Company and has offices in Pensacola and New York and England.

Trial of Inspector McLaughlin

By Southern Associated Press

NEW YORK, April 2. The trial of Police Inspector McLaughlin for receiving bribes, which was set down for this morning in the Court of Oyer and Terminer, has been postponed until April 15. Justice Barrett, who is sitting in Oyer and Terminer, made it clear this morning that there could be no further delay in getting the trial of the inspector under way.

To Attack Canton

By Southern Associated Press

LONDON, April 8. A dispatch from Hong Kong to the Globe says that forty Japanese transports are assembled at the Pescadores, and it is reported that it is intended to man an attack upon Canton. Preparations are actively making to defend that city and torpedoes are being placed at the mouth of the river to prevent the enemy's ships from ascending.

An Unfortunate Suicide

By Southern Associated Press.

Columbia, S. C, April 8. - There was a most unfortunate affair at the state Lunatic Asylum to-day. A white patient named Z. F. Watley, about 45 years of age from Edgefield county, who been confined for thirteen years, committed suicide by hanging, using his suspenders us a rope,

Appomattox Park

By Southern Associated Press

Tallahassee, Fla., April 8. The House today reconsidered its action in killing the resolution asking Congress to purchase Appomattox battle-field for a national park und elect a monument to Gens. Lee and Grant on the spot where the former surrendered.

The resolution was passed by a vote of 56 to 2.

Gov. Marvel Dead

By Southern Associated Press

Wilmington, Del., April 8. – Gov. Marvel died at 9:15 tonight after a lingering illness.

***

"And now ladies and gents, an ad in this esteemed newspaper was inserted immediately below the news

of the passing of the Govenor of Delaware which I might remind you, was our First State," reminded Allen.
***

Won't he look nice with one of Jack Oliver's knobby spring huts, in black or color? He has a large stock to select from and is sure to suit you, at the lowest prices.
Call and be convinced at 111 Main Street. Beauties in Knox's spring styles.
***

Allen's rendition of the ad was completed with a sweeping bow and full swing of his hat to the crowd, whereupon he was given an enthusiastic applause, either for the performance or in appreciation of the death of the politician, which wasn't clear to me, perhaps it was both.

"And now folks, I am sure you will applaud this latest development from the High Court over the efforts of the rascals in Washington to steal your money by way of income tax." Allen beamed as the war whoops and boos filled the air.
***

INCOME TAX IN PART UNCONSTITUTIONAL
The Supreme Court's Decision in the Income Tax Case,
DISSENTING OPINIONS FILED.
The Law is Declared Invalid Taxing Real Estate or Rents Therefrom.
Also Municipal and State Bonds. The Effect of the Decision. New Orders.
By Southern Associated Press.
Washington, April 8. The announcement of the decision of the United States Supreme Court of the income tax was made today in the presence of a

crowded courtroom, the spectators' lobby being thronged to its utmost capacity. Shortly after noon Chief Justice Fuller said, amidst an almost painful stillness: I am charged with the duty of announcing the opinion and judgment of the court in the case of Charles Pollock versus the Farmers' Loan and Trust Company et al."

The opinion began with the constitutionality of direct taxes by the Federal government, which the court held allowable only when great pressure of the extraordinary exigency occurs, and then when taxation is proportionate to the representation. Taxes on real estate belong to the class of direct taxes, and the taxes on the rent or income of real estate, which is the incident of its ownership, belong to the same class. Accordingly this feature of the tax was declared unconstitutional.

The court was further of the opinion that the action of August 15, 1894, is invalid so far as it attempts to levy a tax upon the income derived from municipal bonds.

As a municipal corporation is the representative of the State, - and one of the instrumentalities of the State government, the property and revenues of municipal corporations are not the subjects of federal taxation nor is the income derived from state, county and municipal securities, since taxation on the interest therefrom operates on the power to borrow before it is exercised and has an influence on the contract. Therefore, such a tax is a tax on the power of the States and their instrumentalities to borrow money, and consequently repugnant to the constitution.

Upon each of the other questions argued at the bar, to wit:

1. Whether the void provisions as to rents and income from real estate invalidates the whole act?

2. Whether us to the income from personal property as such, the act is unconstitutional as laying direct taxes.

3. Whether any part of the tax, if not considered as a direct tax is invalid for want of uniformity on either of the grounds suggested? The justices who heard the argument are equally divided and therefore no opinion is expressed.

The result is that the decree of the Circuit Court is reversed and the case remanded, with directions to enter a decree in favor of complainant in respect only of the voluntary payment of the tax on the rents or income of its real estate and that which it holds in trust, and on the income from the municipal bonds owned or so held by it.

Justices Field and White read independent dissenting opinions.

At 2:35 the court concluded the reading of opinions, whereupon the question of the constitutionality of taxation of income from States und municipal bonds the court was unanimously in the negative.

Upon the question of taxation and rents the court stood us follows:

Affirming the Law- -Justices Harlan and White. Against the Law- Chief Justice Fuller, Justices Field, Gray, Brewer, Brown and Shiras.

Upon the general question of the constitutionality of the law, the court is said to be divided its follows: For the Law Justices Harlan, Brewer, Brown, and White. Against the Law:

Chief Justice Fuller, Justices Field, Gray, and Shiras.

The President was informed of the income tax decision shortly after it was rendered by the Supreme Court, and at 1:30 he summoned Secretary Carlisle to the executive mansion and the two discussed the matter for some time.

Other members of the Cabinet dropped in later, among them the Attorney-General. The decision was a disappointment, but the administration will at once issue instructions to collectors of internal revenue to conform to the emasculated law, Secretary Carlisle followed his well-defined custom not to discuss the matter for publication.

Attorney General Olney said the government would not ask for a rehearing, but would accept the decision as rendered. He was not surprised at that portion of it excepting municipal and State bonds from taxation; but expressed the hope that the question of rents might be brought before the court in some other shape, when he entertained the strong belief that the present attitude of the court would be revised.

In the Treasury department, Assistant Secretary Curtis declared that the condition of the Treasury was good, and the revenues would meet current expenses.

CUBAN AFFAIRS

By Southern Associated Press

Havana (Via Key West), April 8. A band of insurgents, found cutting the wires in the Santiago de Cuba District, near Palerma Soriano, was fired upon yesterday by Government troops under Gen. LaChambre. It is reported that one of the insurgent leaders was killed, the wires were repaired, and service between Santiago and Havana is restored,

Insurgent bands of 400 or 500 men each are numerous in the province of Santiago, but the

158

authorities report all quiet in other provinces. A party of eight whites and three Negroes started from here in an omnibus yesterday. The authorities were warned several days ago, and the party was captured six miles outside of Havana. They were armed with revolvers and earned an insurgent flag,

They are now in jail here; it is said they expected others to meet them and intended attacking the barracks of the Civil Guard at Jaruco. Reports of insurgent successes in the interior are denied by authorities here.

Kate Douglas Wiggin as Hostess

The last time I saw her she was acting in the capacity of cordon bleu, of musician und singer, and poetess and humorist and hostess, writes Emma B. Kaufman in on interesting sketch of "The Personality of a Charming Writer" in The Ladies' Home Journal. The feast she gave was a novel one. On the menu cards, it was presented as a country supper and served to the announcement of "The vittles is up."

There were artist's und lawyers and a dramatist and a critic at her board who cooked and served dishes to the rest of us less talented ones. I remember Mrs. Wiggin's venison, which she fried in its own juices in a way that showed that if she had not been a musician and a singer, and a poetess, and a humorist, and a writer, and a reader she might have made her living, and a good one, as a cook. Before we left the table, we were presented with envelopes fittingly addressed. Mr. Laurence Hutton's was inscribed:

To one who hoards curios rather than self,
The gem of the treasure house being himself.
***

Allen paused and looked out the saloon window and saw that the *George Washington* was approaching the wharves of Alexandria, Virginia.

"Folks, we will soon be docking in Alexandria and then on to our overnight stop in the City of Washington. Therefore, we have time for some last items, but popular ones, those of gossip and other items. First...a few obituaries and baseball news."

***

NEWS OF STATE AND CAPITAL

General Matters in Richmond and the Commonwealth at Large.

IN HONOR OF GOV. KEMPER.

The Times' Exposure of Henrico County Election Fraud is Nothing New. An Old Baptist Minister.

Richmond's New Infield.

Mahone's Assignment.

Special Dispatch to the Virginian.

Richmond, Va. April 8. Information has been received hereof the death of Rev. Joseph Walker at Scottsville; he was perhaps the oldest Baptist preacher in Virginia, being about 90 years of age. Mr. Walker was strong and active up to a few weeks ago, when he was taken ill. He was a native of Chesterfield County.

The news of the death of ex-Gov. James L. Kemper was not a surprise here. He had been in poor health for a long lime. Gov. O'Ferrall was not at the Capitol to-day, having gone to Fincastle to attend the funeral of Capt. J. H. H. Figgatt, but the flags on the Capitol will be placed at half-mast in honor of Gov. Kemper's memory. Gen. Kemper was Governor from 1874 to 1878. He leaves two or three children. One son, of whom he was exceedingly proud, died in Norfolk a few years ago.

Gen. Edgar Allan arrived from Washington today and talked to the newspaper reporters about the trust deed which Gen. Mahone executed last week. He has been the General's counsel for a good while back and is familiar with all his affairs. Mahone, he says, is by no means a bankrupt man, but owns property in Washington that will net him probably $300,000. This deed was executed solely to save his Virginia estate from being subjected to the payment of a debt he did not think he owed. The story about Mahone owing Senators and Representatives large sums of money is, Gen. Allan says, pure fabrication.

Mr. Wells, the manager of the Richmond baseball team, has released Pitcher Allen and sent him home. He proved to be too light for this League.

Mr. Wells has signed us a second baseman Fred Hauseman, who during a part of last season played shortstop for the Chicago National League team,

Hauseman is expected here tomorrow.

Hull, who has been playing this position, will probably have to go. Behne will be assigned to third base and McGowan will be kept as a sort of general utility man.

VOTE BUYING IN RECENT ELECTION

The exposure in the *Times* yesterday of vote buying at the late primary in Henrico did not occasion much of a sensation in the County. All the facts were; it is said, pretty well known beforehand. The county committee, I am told, proposes to take no notice of the matter. *As all the candidates were engaged in the purchase of votes,* none of them appear over anxious to ventilate the matter.

***

Hoods Pills cure jaundice, biliousness, sick headache, constipation and all liver ills.

HOODS SARSPARILIA – the great blood purifier!

***

"Folks, that's all the news for this voyage of the *George Washington* which will tie up at Maine Avenue in a few minutes with all manner of conveyance of taxis, buggies and street cars available for your needs in the City of Washington. Thank you for steaming with the Old Bay Line."

Building the steamship John G. Christopher at Wilmington,

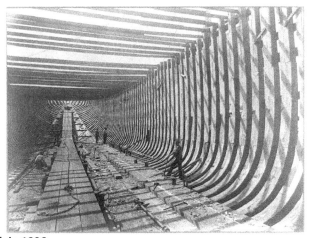

Del. in 1896

CHAPTER SIXTEEN
The Big Dig & a Ride in the Park with TR

My son Charles had been working on the *Washington Herald* for ten years since beginning as a copy boy and runner to fetch and deliver messages between the news desk and reporters on assignments in the Capitol, the White House and their favorite bars. Sometimes those destinations included the favorite brothels of the reporters, which provided further education for the aspiring reporter.

The day that President McKinley had been murdered in New York while attending an exposition found Charles working his fourth year as a full-fledged reporter for the *Herald* on assignments at the White House.

Working as a reporter for my brother's newspaper had been an education unto itself, the defense Charles raised each time his mother began to beat the drums of him attending college. To keep her happy, he enrolled in part-time classes at Georgetown University.

That exposure to learning some aspects of a formal education came in handy for Charles in many ways and one of the first was in being named the new White House reporter for the *Herald* as Roosevelt was sworn in as the new president.

Charles had been covering stories about the Vice President since the Spanish-American War adventures of the Rough Rider, and the editor of the *Herald* believed that the relationship forged over two years prepared him well for the post.

One of Charles's cohorts in the capital city circles of politics and journalists was Archie Butt. Butt had been covering Washington for several southern newspapers,

The Louisville Post, The Atlanta Constitution, The Nashville Banner, The Augusta Chronicle, and The Savannah News.

Becoming part of Archie Butt's weekly poker part enabled Charles also to be privy to inside news of the White House as Butt became Roosevelt's military adviser and then Chief of Staff.

Charles' star at the *Herald* didn't need any help from his uncle the publisher, he had built a solid reputation as digging out news stories, many of which caused heartburn for Roosevelt - especially over the Panama Canal.

The French had been digging the canal in a haphazard way and seemed to be quitting with less than half the job done.

President Roosevelt was a dynamo on any topic he believed in, and this ditch was going to happen. Some wanted the canal to be dug through Nicaragua and abandon the mess left behind by the French in Panama.

Charles worked hard at keeping up with all facets of the story, often earning the ire of his friend Archie Butt. He was occasionally tweaked by the President himself when Charles was invited to go on a horseback ride to Rock Creek Park with the two of them.

While some of the Hearst newspapers were lambasting Roosevelt and accusing him of using public money to pay off big money investors in the failed French effort, many in the nation wanted to see the canal finished. Manufacturers wanted the new shipping route so as to encourage markets on both coasts of the United States, as well as increase world trade.

Charles kept his reporting balanced, keeping the focus on the bargain of having the canal built by America and being a remarkable military advantage.

CHESAPEAKE 1880

American warships could quickly move from one ocean to another with the canal. Freight could move back and forth without the powerful railroads extracting a pound of flesh for each pound of freight. The monopolies were in full force, and Roosevelt was determined to break up the trusts.

There could never have been a better time to be a reporter for a major newspaper in the nation's capital and to be assigned the White House beat. To think my son Charles was a regular at the weekly poker games of the key players in the nation made me burst with pride.

When the stories with his byline burst onto the front page day after day, on the top news of the times, I wasn't the only one who became a regular reader. So did the rest of Washington and across the country as other newspapers carried his news stories.

His younger brothers were now the news readers on the steamships, and they loved to ham it up when reading one of their older brother's news stories. Some of those were repeated at the dinner table at Thanksgiving and Christmas with special emphasis on typographical errors and humorous content.

As the battle to build the Panama Canal raged in Congress, Charles began to meet with a lobbyist who had been working hard with the committees in the House of Representatives that would decide the matter.

Alan Cecil had been an attorney and lobbyist in Washington for twenty-five years and had performed many legal tasks for my companies. Now he was representing those who were arguing for the United States to pay off the French investors and finish the canal.

Following a long day of hearings, Cecil consented to an interview with Charles at the Willard Hotel.

"How is your father?" asked Cecil.

"He is as busy as ever with his businesses and now finds that investments in oil, gas, and telephones have promise," answered Charles. "I never know what is going to get his attention next, I just hope he doesn't get involved in the Canal while I work on this story, I would hate to have him after me as well for reporting something he doesn't like,"

"Has he ever admonished you about one of your stories?" asked Cecil.

"Come to think of it, no, he always tells me how much he learned from them and liked them."

"I suspect that is the only thing you will ever hear from him about your work."

"Well, it's a lot different from my editor and my Uncle John. They raise hell with me on a regular basis, and it's like pulling teeth sometimes to get a story into print without having to jump through a lot of hoops," said Charles.

"All for the better," replied Cecil. "That extra layer of caution and protection makes for a better paper and certainly a better legal position."

"You're right. Now about this canal. I noticed today that the House Commerce Committee seems to be leaning towards building a canal through Nicaragua. You sure don't favor it but can you convince the committee to see it your way?" asked Charles Douglas has he drew on his cigar.

"Odd you should ask me this question today," said Cecil with a laugh. "How about a scoop, young man?"

"I like scoops right well."

"On the way over here to the Willard to meet you I was walking past a stationer's store, and I noticed these commemorative stamps in the window," explained Cecil. "One set in particular caught my eye. They were from Nicaragua and feature a volcano on them, a rather large volcano and a well-done piece of art, I might add. In fact, I liked them so much I bought all twenty-five sets the stationer had in stock and inquired if any of his competitors had any. He told me where to find them, and I have bought another fifty sets."

"I doubt you are all of a sudden interested in promoting Nicaragua."

"Charles that is exactly what I am going to do. This very evening I am preparing a letter to each member of the House Commerce Committee. I will include a set of these Volcano stamps and underlined in my letter that should the committee decide to dig a canal through Nicaragua that an eruption could shut down the canal once it's finished and become the biggest boondoggle the nation has ever seen."

"Amazing," Charles noted with a laugh.

"Son, here is a set of the stamps for you to go with your story that I trust you will go back to your office and write tonight."

"Mr. Cecil, tonight is my regular poker game with Maj. Butt at the White House, but I suspect I can gamble a bit later after I do a story for the morning paper."

***

Culebra Cut in the Panama Canal.

VOLCANO ROUTE COULD CLOBBER CANAL

By Charles Douglas

The Washington Herald

WASHINGTON, D.C. - The House Commerce committee is considering a route for the trans-ocean canal currently under consideration that would involve building the canal through Nicaragua and close to active volcanos.

A lobbyist for those favoring buying out the French investors, Alan Cecil, of Washington, has provided the *Washington Herald* with a full set of commemorative stamps issued by Nicaragua which proudly boasts of the nation's volcanos.

Cecil has provided each member of the committee with a letter warning of the dire consequences of an eruption once a canal is built through that country.

The vote on the final decision is scheduled for today.

***

Charles would never have known it, but I was one of those who had bought stock in a company prepared to provide the excavation equipment needed to finish the canal. I was sure glad to see his story appear on the wires across the country.

***

House Committee Commits to Panama Route for Canal

By Charles Douglas

The Washington Herald

WASHINGTON, D.C. --- Following the disclosure of the possible route of the trans-ocean canal through Nicaragua, which has active volcanos, the House Commerce Committee voted 38-2 to recommend to the full House to pass House Bill 222. The bill that will enable the President to purchase ownership of the

Panama Canal from a group of French investors and fund the completion of the construction.

The entire project could be completed in ten years, predicted White House Chief of Staff Maj. Archibald Butt.

While some Senators oppose the bill, the full House, and the Senate are expected to pass a bill, and $50 million will be appropriated to buy out the French.

***

"Charles, we missed you at last night's poker game," said Archie Butt as the White House butler escorted Charles Douglas into the Blue Room, the official poker venue of the executive mansion. "Of course from this morning's paper, I could see that you were busy with Cecil. The President liked your article too, and he left word to summon him once you arrived tonight."

"I sure didn't dress for meeting the president tonight, Archie; you could have given me some warning."

"Don't be an old fogey, Charles, the President doesn't give a hoot about your attire. Now sit down and pull up a glass, he is as happy as a lark and for today only, you are the favorite reporter of the President of the United States. Just don't expect that status to be permanent."

"Young man," boomed President Roosevelt as he entered the room, "That was one fine newspaper article and I liked it so much I sent the Secret Service out to buy 50 copies of the *Herald*. Of course, the money came from my personal funds, not the taxpayers."

"Thank you, sir, it's always a pleasure to be able to report on a story that enjoys appreciation from our readers," Charles noted as he nodded to the President in acceptance for the compliment.

"Now, young man, we are going to have a drink and I have a question for you?"

"Thank you, sir, what is your question?"

"Can you ride a horse?"

"Yessiree, I'm a country boy at heart and by heritage."

"Good, be here at 10 am sharp tomorrow as after I meet with my cabinet on the Panama Canal, you are going to join Archie and me on a horseback ride through Rock Creek Park and we'll circle back to the White House where I wish you will be my guest for lunch," said the President.

"Certainly sir, may I have this ride be on the record?"

"Absolutely, I wouldn't have it any other way."

***

With several mounted police both ahead and behind the Presidential riding party, the trip was uneventful until the President's horse reared when spooked by a rattlesnake in Rock Creek Park.

Maj. Butt, who had become accustomed to wearing a sidearm when horseback riding with the President each week, drew down on the snake and killed it. Dead.

The President had been thrown from his horse but was unhurt.

"I have had other sudden meetings with the terra firma, and this old Rough Rider expects I will have more," exclaimed President Roosevelt.

The ride continued without further excitement and upon returning to the White House, Charles Douglas joined Butt and the President for a long lunch, an exchange of stories and a cigar.

Charles took a pass on the bourbon and left to go back to the *Herald* to write the story of the day with the President.

***

PISTOL PACKING AIDE NAILS RATTLER THAT UNSEATED ROUGH RIDER

By Charles Douglas
The Washington Herald

WASHINGTON, D. C. --- The same day that President Roosevelt won a significant victory in Congress on the Panama Canal proposal, the old Rough Rider was thrown from his horse. The mishap occurred when his trusty mount was spooked by a rattlesnake.

The snake was quickly terminated by Major Archibald Butt, who was escorting the President on a ride through Washington's Rock Creek Park.

Major Butt had taken to wearing a side arm to provide extra protection to the President, who has declared that he will maintain a public presence in spite of the assassination of his predecessor.

The President was unhurt and finished his day with a meeting with administration officials on planning the next steps in implementing the decision to fund the Panama Canal proposal.

***

Charles often was included in other White House events, and the inside scoops in the Herald made my brother John's newspaper the paper of record for the nation's capital. My son Charles had become the city's top reporter and his mother finally decided that he might make something of himself without a college education.

***

President Sets New Record for Receptions
By Charles Douglas
The Washington Herald

WASHINGTON, D.C. --- At a reception for Prince Henry of England last night; Maj. Archibald Butt assisted the President in setting a most unusual record – that of greeting 1,280 persons in one hour. All of them were introduced in a flawless rendition of memory by Maj. Butt to the President and Prince Henry.

Major Butt is well known to the Washington diplomatic, congressional and business circles, and those relationships allowed him to provide a remarkable reminder of the importance of his skills since becoming President Roosevelt's top aide.

Maj. Butt first attained the notice of the President due to a series of articles he wrote on the care of Army mules and horese in tropical conditions. Of particular interest to the President due to his own Army service and the nation's Armies of Occupation in the Philippines and Cuba.

***

As the Panama Canal work got underway after the French were paid off and got out of the way, the materials needed to finish the canal began to flow to the scene.

Charles accompanied the President on two trips to Panama to inspect the work that was underway. His reports and dispatches back to the City of Washington were read with great interest and sent out on the wires across the nation.

Charles hoped to be on the first ship to pass through the canal when it was completed in a few years. He told me he would be carrying the commemorative Nicaraguan stamps given him by Alan Cecil.

While far away the Panama Canal was becoming a reality, a canal closer to home became a project that shipping interests were keenly interested, that of enlarging the existing canal to connect the Chesapeake Bay and the Delaware Bay to a free and open waterway. President Roosevelt saw the advantages and soon appointed a commission to get the ball rolling.

I was always aware of the competing interests of shipping and railroads and was heavily invested in both, making for some interesting conflicts of interests.

Puck Magazine cartoon is showing railroad interests attempting to block a decision to build the Panama Canal.

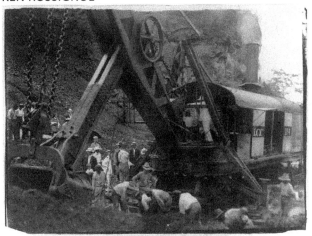

President Roosevelt on a steam shovel in Panama Canal.

President Roosevelt gets first-hand report.

CHAPTER SEVENTEEN
The Great Baltimore Fire

Fires that swept many big cities led to important changes in building codes, fire prevention efforts and great suffering. So was the story of Baltimore in 1904.

Old Bay Line was virtually unscathed because most of our investments in steamships and my other investments in railroads involved rolling stock and other movable assets. Our headquarters on Pratt Street was a different matter.

Four members of our staff who were working when the fire roared to life were injured as they joined the effort to fight the blazing inferno.

Our company records had been in a lead vault and were undamaged.

As the fire spread towards the harbor, the steamships that were in port joined the dozens of other craft in cutting their lines and heading out into the river to outrun the flames. Sparks blew across the harbor and ignited some vessels that couldn't outrun the holocaust.

The fire did what the fleet of the mightiest power in the world, the British Royal Navy, could not do in 1814 – scorch Baltimore with much of it burned to the ground. The British were successful in burning the major public buildings of Washington but were stopped at Fells Point when their invasion fell short as the bombardment in the harbor failed to silence the guns of Fort McHenry.

Salvatore D'Alessandro had been working as a Baltimore Police Officer for but a year. He was working the night shift and patrolling near Camden Yards when the fire began. Fire engines were soon clanging loudly as they rushed past the young officer in the dimly lit street.

B.&.O. Flyer and Crew that Carried WASH'N FIREMEN TO BALT'O IN 31 Minutes, fastest Run Ever Made.

The calls went out to neighboring towns and cities and soon fire engines and firefighters were arriving from as far away as Washington, D.C.

One of those who join the train full of firefighters, engines and equipment was Charles Douglas, to cover the story for readers of *The Washington Herald.*

Charles Douglas arrived in Camden Yards on the special Baltimore & Ohio, which set a record in living up to its name and 'flying' to Baltimore in 31 minutes.

Interior View of Public Store House, showing stone pillars crumbled by heat

The B & O sent all other trains onto sidings and gave the Flyer the green light to fly to Baltimore.

Arriving on the scene, the first person Douglas met was Baltimore Police Officer D'Alessandro, who he knew from reporting on the trial of a Baltimore sea captain who murdered one of his crew the previous year.

"Sal, where did the fire start?"

"Downtown, is the best I can tell right now but there doesn't appear to be any way to stop it, the fire engines from all around Baltimore are arriving but as soon as they try to hook up to a hydrant, the arriving firemen are finding that their hoses don't fit our hydrants," related D'Alessandro.

Charles Douglas began to walk closer towards the growing fire, stopping to dip his handkerchief in a horse trough to wet it and cover his face.

Engines clanked by with bells ringing as firemen began the fruitless task of trying to find a hydrant that might be of a matching size for their hoses.

One fire company from Ellicott City began to sort through other fire companies in an attempt to stretch compatible hoses to the harbor and pump water up to engines that were making some headway.

Firemen from nearly two dozen cities had responded to the Great Baltimore Fire of Feb. 7th and 8th only to find out what the firefighters of Washington and Ellicott City learned; few of their hoses fit each other's couplings or the hydrants.

Much was learned about fighting fires on those two days. Unfortunately, those who had been giving warnings about the great need to update firefighting equipment had been ignored. There were over 600 different sizes and types of fire hose couplings in use, which made virtually useless all of the fire companies that rushed to the assistance of Baltimore.

The young reporter made his way through the ruins to a section of the city untouched by the fire, the area known as Little Italy.

As he walked along past several taverns and cafes, Officer D'Alessandro called out his name from the doorway of a bakery.

"You must be hungry by now; step on in here to my family's bakery, its dinner time and we have plenty," said Sal.

The outside of the three-story building was made of red brick, the same as most of the tidy row houses and stores along the street. The smoke and soot from the fire had left a coating of ashes across the city and people were everywhere with brooms and carts cleaning up the neighborhood.

"Thank you, I am starving, as I sure didn't have time to grab my lunch pail before jumping onto the Baltimore Flyer to get up here yesterday and then I slept in a warehouse down by the dock last night. I don't think you'll want me stinkin' up your kitchen."

As they began to enter the bakery, the Baltimore Morgue wagon drove by on the way to Pratt Street.

"Believe it or not that is the first one I have seen, so far, I expect there will more call for them as we go through the burned out buildings," noted Sal. "I have to go back to work at midnight as I am posted downtown to keep out looters."

"Is it true that the police have been given orders to shoot to kill?"

"I wouldn't doubt it but as yet, it hasn't been ordered, but I'll find out at roll call," said Sal.

The Hurst Building where the fire began and destroyed much of downtown Baltimore.

A police officer guards the ruins of a jewelry store in the downtown district after the fire was extinguished. Library of Congress

Charles Street during the great Baltimore fire.

Washington Engine No. 6 in action in Baltimore fire.

Burgander Bros. at 115 West Street in Baltimore after the fire.

Ellicott City train station in 1893.

The burned out downtown business district from across the harbor in Baltimore, Md.

Carrolton Hotel ruins at Light and German Street in Baltimore, Md., following the disastrous fire.

A store at a wharf along the Chesapeake. F. C. Yohn

CHAPTER EIGHTEEN

The Peddler and the Priest

As the *George Washington* steamed south from Chesapeake Beach towards Cove Point, the balmy day became slightly less humid and Father John Mattingly walked out to the railing of the steamboat and inhaled the fresh air. As the young priest, returning from his ordination at the Sacred Heart Cathedral in Baltimore, gazed upon the shoreline which revealed the mouth of the Patuxent River; he wondered about his first assignment back in his home county of St. Mary's.

"Good afternoon, Father," said the stocky passenger who walked up next to him and joined him at the rail.

"Top of the day to you sir," replied Mattingly. "Are you headed to Washington or is your stop coming up soon?"

"My stop is always the next stop," said Millison with a laugh. "I am a peddler, Father, I bring all manner of goods to each landing and can arrange shipment of larger items, usually within a week as long as the warehouse in Baltimore has the merchandise in stock."

"I'm John Mattingly, sir, glad to meet a peddler in person," Mattingly said with an outreached hand.

"I'm Samuel Millison at least that is the name of the peddler from whom I bought my business, my name actually is Hiram Goldberg."

"Why did you take the name of the peddler?"

"Father, it was easier that way. All the farmers and stores on the route of the steamship that Samuel bought from knew that Millison treated them fairly and never sold them a bill of goods so I decided that if I bought a fine hardware store on Pratt Street with a venerated name, I would have kept the name of the store so why not keep the name of the peddler?"

"Makes sense to me, Samuel, so I shall call you by that name, at least until you sell your peddler's business!"

"Thank you Father, do I take it that I have your blessing?"

"Samuel, you shall be my first to bless as this is my first trip away from being ordinated as a priest, I am on my way to where my family lives and my first assignment in a parish."

The priest then made the sign of the cross and blessed the peddler as the steamboat passed down the Chesapeake.

Millison became a blessed Jew that day and it began a long association he and his family would have with many Catholics in the future. Free to practice his faith, the religion of his ancestors, unmolested. Traveling from Lithuania and fleeing persecution from one country in Europe to another, Millison was able to book passage on a liner to Baltimore.

Once he landed in Baltimore; Millison had walked along a few city blocks until he came to a dry goods store operated by Mortimer Millison. A sign in the window advertised "Peddler Business for Sale – Inquire Within" .

Millison opened the door to the ringing of bells to gain the attention of the proprietor. In the back of the store, Mortimer Millison waved and said, "step right back here, and I will be glad to help you as soon as I untangle myself from these yard goods."

"I saw your sign in the window," said Samuel.

"This is your lucky day."

By the end of the day, Samuel had arranged to buy the stock of the peddler route that circled the Bay. He agreed to make payments to Mortimer who explained that his brother had owned the peddler route but was killed when a team of horses spooked by a fire engine bolted and he was run down by the wagon the previous week.

"Oy vey, vat you going to do? First the fire and then this tragic end to my brother. He had worked hard and built a good business, had customers all around the Chesapeake. He would board a steamboat and not return for two weeks. He would fill orders and ship them to landings for pickup and then he would go out again to travel the Bay and rivers to sell more items," explained Mortimer.

"You need to use his name too, it's okay, he's not using it anymore and his customers trusted his name."

Cedar Point Lighthouse following years of deterioration from weather and vandals after it was taken out of service due to erosion caused by gravel mining.

Forever more, Goldberg was known as Samuel Millison. But he named his son Hiram, which had not only been his name but that of his grandfather. His father's name was Ezra and had been killed by the Czar's army as they swept through the small town where his family lived.

There were few places in Europe where Jews were welcome and he had heard of this city of Baltimore where it was said that not only could Jews live in peace, but there was a prevalent sense of tolerance towards his brethren.

Soon Samuel was making his monthly trips to Millison's store on Pratt Street to turn in his orders and have a wagon loaded to take to the wharf and loaded on his steamboat so he could make his next trip.

When arriving in Baltimore, he stayed in a room above the store; the same as Mortimer's brother had done. It all made sense.

What also made sense was for Samuel to rent a wagon from a farmer at each steamboat landing and travel the countryside selling to farmers in the area with the goods he unloaded from the steamboat.

That is how he came to Pearson, Maryland.

Millison had been selling his goods to the store at Pearson, which consisted of a church, St. Nicholas, two stores and a blacksmith shop run by two brothers, Webster, and Ernest Bell.

After a year of calling on Jarboe's store, he learned that old Merton Jarboe had died, and his son was off in the Navy with no intention of returning to operate the country store. Thus the widow of Jarboe, herself in ill health, was glad to accept an offer from Sam to purchase the store.

This time, Millison decided to change the name on the store to his own, at least to his American name and the sign on the store went up with "Millison's Dry Goods, Hardware & Tavern".

Millison sold his peddler's business to a cousin who had arrived from Lithuania, and he brought another acquaintance with him from Baltimore; his new wife Martha, the daughter of Mortimer.

Martha Millison became well known in the area for her mastery of cooking Southern Maryland Stuffed

Hams and supporting the public school system as she had been educated as a teacher in Baltimore.

***

The young priest caught a ride on the back of the wagon from Millstone Landing, which dropped him off on the Three Notch Road. The priest then began walking until a wagon stopped and offered him a ride.

"Father, it's a long walk to wherever you're headed but easier upon this buckboard," offered Johnny Ridgell as he chewed on a pipe.

"Bless you for your kind offer, may I know your name?"

"Yep, it's Johnny Ridgell, and thank you for your blessing, I need all of them I can get due to my inordinate amount of swearing," said Johnny with a laugh.

"The Lord hears you in any language you use, as long as you keep him in mind."

He was soon dropped off at a small stone church with fields nearby and a small cemetery to one side. With less than fifty graves around the priest wondered if parishioners were either few, particularly healthy or if the church was recently built. He soon learned that two out the three were true and that large families existed in this area full of Catholics, just like his home parish of St. Francis Xavier on the distant shores of the Breton Bay on the far side of St. Mary's County.

Unlike the church where he was raised which had a large mission house next to it as a residence for priests who served several parishes, his first assignment had a simple frame cottage nearby to serve as the rectory.

Father Mattingly also thought about the great cook at St. Francis Xavier and thought if only he had been assigned at that wonderful church. The bishop had been firm that being assigned to a nearby parish in his home county was about as accommodating that the Archdiocese would be towards its new priest.

He walked over to the frame cottage and was greeted by a large colored woman who answered the door.

"My goodness, look at you, full of dust and grime and ready to walk into my house like that," said Lulu Mae Curtis. "Not on your life, now get yourself out on the back porch and take a bath, and I'll take in your bags and find you some clean clothes. No sir, priest or no priest, you sure ain't gonna make this house a mess, now git on with you if y'all expect to be sitting down to a good meal anytime soon."

As the priest walked around to the rear of the cottage, he could catch the aroma of what must have been fried chicken escaping out the kitchen window. He spotted a tub and jugs of water and figured that he just might have a great place to eat after all as while his vows called for a celibate life, nothing ruled out good eating.

As he settled down into the tub of air-temperature water, Lulu kicked open the kitchen door with her foot and walked over with a large pot of hot water and dumped it over his head.

The temperature was not hot enough to scald but warm enough to show she meant business about seeing to it he was presentable for dinner.

"Don't forget to scrub behind your ears," scolded Lulu," I've had plenty of practice makin' sure young 'uns get cleaned up so you're not gonna fool me, priest or not priest. Even a Jesuit."

CHESAPEAKE 1880

This Jesuit Mission House at Compton, Md. served several parishes of the Washington Diocese. THE CHESAPEAKE TODAY photo

Chapter Nineteen

The Terra Cotta Wreck of B & O No. 66

The tragic wreck of a fast train into the rear of a Baltimore and Ohio passenger train stopped on the main line of the railroad where it enters Washington, D. C. on Dec. 30, 1906 killed as many as 53 persons, in first reports from the scene. Later counts of the dead put the figure at 43. Many more were injured.

The cause of the crash was important in understanding why it took place, how to assign blame and accountability for those responsible and how to prevent such wrecks in the future.

My investments in the B & O Railroad, as well as two other railroads made my interest in the cause of the crash keen; as well as the fact that among the dead and injured were people that I knew.

Many train wrecks around the nation had been assigned to the deficiencies of the block signal system, with many fearing that the next train trip they undertook might be their last. Such conditions were intolerable to continue, and I was as interested as anyone, due to train travel not only being an important part of my investments but one of the chief ways my family and I traveled.

Therefore, I followed every detail of the coroner's inquest into the Terra Cotta wreck through the newspaper coverage.

First, the living and the dead of Train No. 66 as reported in the *Washington Times* on Dec. 31, 1906:

LIST OF THE DEAD
IDENTIFIED

Mrs. M. E. BAINES died in private home at Terra Cotta

J. A. and S. L. BOND, no address found

COMMODORE .P BROWN, identified by pay envelope containing 95 cents.

EDWARD M. BELT, seven-year-old son of Dr. E. Oliver Belt Washington

DON M. CARR Kensington Md.

0. P. DAILEY minister from Newark, Ohio Rural Route No. 2

Dr. E. GAITHER HARRIS, dentist, 1336 New York Avenue

GEORGE HIGBEE seven-year-old son of Harry Higbee

Prof. T. J. KING Kensington., Md., organist at Wesleyan M. E. Church and statistician at Naval Observatory

P. A. KELLY engineer at the Capitol.

J. T. KELLY Kensington Md., motorman

Miss MAY LIPPOLD, sister-in-law of Harry Higbee Bureau of Printing

A. LEE LOWE, 1212 LOWE 1212 F. Street, Columbia Phonograph Company

Mrs. MOORE and one-year-old baby

Mrs. MERKLAND

THOMAS METZ, New York Transfer, corner Eighth Avenue and Forty-Ninth Street

Mrs. M S PERRMANN, North Takoma, D. C.

Miss REEVES, Takoma, D. C.

NORMAN RODGERS, 30 years, Marion, Ind.

LILY D. SCHAEFER

JOHN WRIGHT died at Hospital.

UNIDENTIFIED

Eight-year-child.

Girl, 22, red skirt and gray tourists coat.

Woman, 35, blue coat and black skirt.

Woman, 20, plaid shirtwaist, belt with initials: "U. N. S." and "H. M. S."

Woman, 20, red skirt and white lace waist.

Woman, 40, tan coat, black skirt, two garnet rings.

Girl, 18, green dress Cornell College pin.

Boy, with pass for Mrs. J. A. McCaghey, and son wife and son of chief clerk of general superintendent, Baltimore and Ohio.

Mangled body of a man.

Boy letter M on clothes mangled remains.

Boy ten years old,

Colored woman.

White man mangled beyond recognition.

Woman, 30, blue coat black skirt.

Child mangled beyond recognition.

Girl, 20, "S" embroidered on handkerchief, brown suit.

Woman, 30, checked shirtwaist, tan coat.

Four decapitated bodies of men and women

Child, girl, about 13.

Woman wearing wedding ring, " P. C. to "M. C. L." black skirt and white shirt waist.

Woman, 35, large wedding ring.

Child; white.

Child; colored.

Colored woman died at Providence Hospital

LIST OF THE INJURED

ROY ADLER Poolesville, Md., right arm broken

Miss FANNY AUSTIN, 1802 D. Street southeast

Engineer ANDERSON, of train No 66

SAMMY AUSTIN, colored, 36-years-old, 802 D. Street, southeast

DISTRICT ATTORNEY D. W. BAKER, 1523 T. street northwest, crushed heel, badly bruised about face; walked to Brookland and was treated at a pharmacy by Dr. Brooks.

LOUIS BALDWIN, Washington, internal injuries.

BERTHA BEAZE, 419 New York Avenue

FRANK B. BOBLITZ, Frederick, Md., scalp wound and jaw broken.

LUCILLE CAMPHER.

Mrs. DON L CARR, Kensington.

LUCILE COMP, 6-years-old.

Miss ROSIE CROSS, Seneca, telephone.

Mrs. R. J. COOLEY, 215 New Jersey Avenue.

HOWELL CHAMBERS, 1008 Eleventh street northwest.

JOHN DICKENS, Park road.

CORNELIUS ECKHART, auditor of the Washington Star.

RICHARD F. ELGIN.

CHARLES T. FAGAN, 23 years-old, Frederick Md.

B. FRANKLIN, brakeman, badly cut and crushed condition serious.

FRED HEISER, Takoma Park.

C. C. HOMILLER, Seneca, Md.

CATHERINE B. HUGHES.

HUGHES 1438 Corcoran Street NW

W. C. JOHNSON, General Agent, United States Express Co. arm broken.

LYSLE JONES, Washington.

Mrs. JOHN KENLOW.

JOHN A. KUNLO, grocer, 18 P. street northwest.

JOHN KAUHLER, Washington, both legs broke.

HENRY KRISS, Takoma Park.

E. B. LADD, brakeman, 255 R Street northwest.

B. N. MAYWOOD, Alexandria County, Va.

J. A. McCLING, 25-years-old, 408 M Street northwest.

H. O. Miller.

JOHN MERTUNE, M street northwest.

Mr. and Mrs. C. L. MOORE

Mrs. A. MOON, Sheridan.

CHESTER L. MOORE, Sheridan.

ELIZABETH PERRIMAN, Takoma.

C. A. PROCTOR, 321 P. street northwest.t

HENRY REED, Terra Cotta.

Miss JEANNETTE REID, Washington.

C. R. RANBURG, Frederick.

B. S. SEGGS, Washington.

ADA SMITH.

Mrs. ELIZABETH TEIRAN Takoma Park.

HARVEY THOMAS, wife and son, 63 L. Street

Mr. Thomas cut about face; Mrs. Thomas cut about face and badly bruised; boy not in injured.

JOHN WILKINS, ankle broken and head cut

JOHN WRIGHT, colored, 50 years, 850 Stockholm Street, Baltimore.

EDWARD WILLIAMS, colored, 1154 Nineteenth street, Washington; came to the city on the electric car and had wounds about face dressed.

ALBERT YORK, Woodburn, D.C.

Unidentified Injured:

Two-year-old child at Freedmen's Hospital.

Four-year-old child at Freedmen's Hospital.

Two unknown men at Providence Hospital.

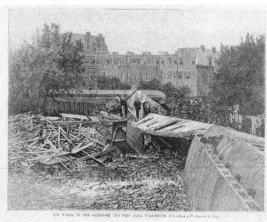

QUARTER IN WRECK INQUIRY
FOR B. & O. MEN
Second Day of Inquiry into Terra Cotta Wreck
Show Road Gave Victims Only Second Thought

The Washington Times

WASHINGTON, D.C. - JAN 3, 1907 — The Inquiry as to the cause of and responsibility for the frightful catastrophe on the Baltimore and Ohio Railroad at Terra Cotta on Sunday, was resumed by Coroner Nevitt in the "Firefighter" headquarters this morning shortly before 11 o'clock.

Corner Nevitt wielded the probe as never before during his term of office and allowed the Baltimore and Ohio officials no quarter. They made evasive replies to his queries, repeated their answers time and again, and moved nervously on the witness stand, but the fusillade of questions was kept up by Dr. Nevitt until he got the reply which he knew to be correct.

What Dr. Nevitt wanted to know was why the relief train was delayed at University for thirteen minutes and a passenger train was allowed to pass it on the way to

Terra Cotta, and why the Baltimore and Ohio officials took it upon themselves to arrange for the removal of the dead before he had seen the bodies.

SHIFT RESPONSIBILITY

Responsibility for these two occurrences was shifted by one witness to another.

Coroner Nevitt finally became exasperated and said to the jury: "I went to the Baltimore and Ohio station immediately after hearing of the wreck and asked about how I would get to Terra Cotta. A man named Robey said he did not know, unless I went in an ambulance or a patrol wagon. That was all the satisfaction I, the Coroner, could get at the station and finally I ordered a relief train sent out by railroad and after some delay the train was started."

Who let the passenger train pass the relief train was not learned.

What occasioned the delay in starting the relief train is unknown.

Commissioners McFarland and West were present again today and suggested many questions for Dr. Nevitt to ask. James M. Watson and I. M. Walter of the Interstate Commerce Commission; Assistant District Attorneys Turner and Proctor, and many other attorneys were present.

INQUEST LAGGING

The inquest lagged and dragged on listlessly until after noon.

Three witnesses were called but did not answer. They were Eggleston, Kelly, and McCauley. They will probably answer this afternoon.

Assistant trainmaster J. T. Carr went on the stand when the hearing was resumed today. He was a difficult witness for the Coroner. He appeared nervous and excitable and could tell but little other than wheat he found in dispatches sent by himself and others.

Carr had to be relieved by Train Dispatcher Dent, who was called for the purpose of making some elucidations regarding the delay and presumption of authority to move the dead. Little was learned from him.

The crowd of spectators was much smaller than yesterday, and there was breathing space in the little room.

Assistant Trainmaster J. T. Carr of the Baltimore and Ohio, took the stand at 10:30 o'clock this morning. He was the first witness.

Doctors Are Ordered

He read a telegram by O. H. Hobbs, the superintendent of the Baltimore division of the road. It was "Get all the doctors you can and rush them special to Terra Cotta; 96 is wrecked, and passengers hurt." The time of the dispatch was 6:48 Sunday night.

Witness read another dispatch in which he was ordered to take an operator and linemen to Terra Cotta in order to establish telegraphic communication.

"I went to the Baltimore and Ohio station and found Mr. Robey had a relief train already made up. I don't know what time the train left the station. We had nine doctors and a number of assistants. We arrived about 7:45. We left at 8:49 and arrived at the station at 9:12. Meanwhile, I had telegraphed to Mr. Robey from Terra Cotta to get every doctor, ambulance and wagon he could and rush them out to Terra Cotta.

Consulting a sheet, Mr. Carr found that the relief train left the station at 8:29 and arrived at University at 7:29 and Terra Cotta was reached at 8:32.

Met the Engine

"Did you meet the engine of 66 and one or two coaches at Terra Cotta as you were going to the scene of the wreck?"

"I met the engine and cars about thirty yards this side of Terra Cotta."

"By what authority, official or moral, did that engineer come to Washington?"

"He was running on his schedule."

"Irrespective of the wreck and the fact that the cars might have been used to bring the dead and the injured to the city?"

"If we had kept those cars there and bundled the injured into them before the arrival of the doctors and stimulants, more of them would have died."

Coroner Nevitt has information that one injured man was brought to the city on the cars that could have carried 100 or more.

"Why did you summon those wagons and ambulances?"

"To carry away the dead."

"Ever hear of a body being moved from the track before the Coroner had seen it?"

"No sir."

Witnesses then said he ordered the wagons to have them ready when the Coroner permitted.

Mr. Carr read several reports, in which the extent of damage to the railroad equipment was reported.

One dispatch contained the information that the Engineer Nagle, of 96, said:

"We were struck as soon as we stopped at Terra Cotta."

Engineer Hildebrand and Conductor Hoffmeier said:

"We got a double green signal at Silver Springs. There was no signal at Takoma."

***

MAY SHIFT BLAME ON THE RAILROAD
Coroner Investigates Cause of Terra Cotta Wreck
BLOCK SYSTEM PROBED
Searching Questions Put to Company Officials
Evidence shows that the Engineer Was Not Looking for Red Lights.
Operator Phillips on Duty for Twelve Hours – Agents of the Interstate Commerce Commission on Hand at the Inquest.

Testimony of a startling character, throwing many interesting sidelights upon the Baltimore and Ohio Railroad's block system on the Metropolitan branch, was given at the first hearing of the coroner's inquest yesterday.

It tends to shift the weight of suspicion from the shoulders of the engineer and the crew of the extra train that caused Sunday's wreck at Terra Cotta to the shoulders of those men responsible for the continuance of the day operator system such as practiced at the Takoma Park signal station. An inquest was held at the headquarters of the Firefighter on the river front. The inquest was adjourned until 10 o'clock in the morning.

The hearing was devoted to the examination f the three officials of the railroad – O. H. Hobbs, division superintendent; C. W. Galloway, general superintendent of transportation of the entire Baltimore and Ohio system, and Thomas F. Dent, train dispatcher in charge of the Metropolitan Branch at the time of the wreck.

With deliberation and in carefully worded phrases the railroad officials answered the volley of questions shot at them by Coroner J. Ramsey Nevitt, and at the close of the day's session the following salient points had been made clear:

Phillips Works Twelve Hours

That Operator Milton W. Phillips, of the Takoma block, is customarily off duty from 6:30 pm until 6:30 am.

That at 6:30 pm in the Takoma block becomes ordinarily inoperative for the night, thus making one block of the stretch between Silver Springs and University.

That at 7 pm the operator at University is supposed to go home, thus making his block inoperative and making one block of the track between Silver Springs and the Rhode Island avenue tower.

That the Silver Springs and Rhode Island avenue signal towers remain in operation twenty-four hours daily.

That when a block becomes inoperative no lights are displayed, and the engineers, taking their signals from the operative towers, pass the dead stations with only the ordinary carefulness, and in no more expectancy of signals than when approaching stations where no telegraph operators are employed.

That the engineer of the "extra" running behind the wrecked passenger train Sunday night passed the block between Silver Springs and Takoma at 6:28 o'clock.

That Operator Phillips, still being on duty, must have notified the operator at Silver Springs that the passenger No. 66 had passed into the University block before the Silver Springs operator allowed the extra to clear for Takoma.

That Phillips' customary term of duty expired while the extra, No. 2120, was still running between Silver Spring and Takoma.

That under those circumstances he should have remained on duty – under and unprinted but supposedly rigid rule – and held No. 2020 until the operator at University should have notified him that No. 66 had passed into the University – Rhode Island avenue block, which he is said to have done.

That Phillips should have exposed a red target as a stop signal to the oncoming extra, which he is said to have done.

That Engineer Hildebrand, of 2120, is instructed by no rule to expect that Phillips was still at his post at 6:31, the time that 2120 passed Takoma.

Did Not Expect Signals

That when he is placed on the stand, his defense will be based principally on the claim that he was not to expect signals at Takoma, and that, seeing none, he proceeded with his train.

That this is the first severe test of the "day operator" system, and that apparently, the contingency of a train entering the Takoma block two minutes before Phillips was to leave duty, with a more slowly moving train but a short distance ahead, has not been adequately provided for in the rules and regulations of the railroad.

That had the Takoma station been one operating twenty-four hours, the accident could scarcely have happened inasmuch as Engineer Hildebrand would then surely have been expecting a signal of some sort, and under the rules would have stopped to investigate had he seen no signals.

That Hildebrand has always been regarded at one of the most careful and valuable engineers in the Baltimore and Ohio service.

That the average speed of train 2120 between Silver Spring and Terra Cotta was about twenty-five miles an hour.

That the crew of train No. 66, even if ignorant of the fact that No. 2120 was following closely, were under no obligation or orders to take extra precautions against a rear-end collision while at Terra Cotta.

Investigation Is to Be Thorough

That the investigation by the coroner and other District officials is to be the most thorough was made apparent early in yesterday's proceedings. The examination of the witnesses produced was deliberate and searching. With a carefulness and regard to detail that should satisfy the most exacting. Coroner Nevitt, assisted by Commissioners West and Macfarland and Assistant District Attorney Charles H. Turner, questioned the witnesses upon every phase of the subject upon which they could furnish any information tending to aid the jury in reaching its verdict fixing the responsibility of the disaster. Under the law, the coroner alone could directly question the witnesses. The session lasted from 10:40 o'clock in the morning until nearly 5 in the afternoon with a recess for luncheon of three-quarters of an hour.

Especial import was lent the occasion by the presence of two representatives of the Interstate Commerce Commission – James M. Watson, chief of the division safety appliances, and L. M. Walter, an attorney, employed by the Federal government to prosecute cases of violations of the rules governing the use of these safety devices took copious notes of the proceedings and served subpoenas on the witnesses summoning them to appear at the first hearing, Friday morning of the inquiry to be made by the commission.

Deputy Coroner Dr. L. H. Glazebrook assisted Coroner Nevitt, and Attorney W. J. Colbert, resident counsel of the Baltimore and Ohio Railroad, was present to listen to testimony in the interest of his clients. Assistant District Attorney Turner was accompanied by James M. Proctor and Harvey Given, of the district attorney's office. Corporation Counsel E. H. Thomas sat beside him in suggesting questions to be put by the coroner to the witnesses. Attorney Harry E. Davis, former district attorney, and Charles Bendheim, retained by the brotherhood of railroad men to defend the crew of the extra, were also present.

Witnesses to be Kept Apart

During the examination only the witnesses on the stand were allowed in the room, the other witnesses and the guarded trainmen were being kept in an ante-room until called for.

Dr. Edgar Snowton, the physician that performed the autopsy on the body of Prof. T. J. King, of Kensington, was the first witness called. He described the condition of the body and ascribed death to fracture of the skull. Coroner Nevitt explained to the jury that in cases where more than one person is killed through the same cause, the inquest is held over one body, and the verdict is understood to include all.

Division Superintendent Hobbs was then called. Mr. Hobbs made a splendid witness. Gravely, and with due deliberation, he answered to the best of his ability all the questions asked, evading direct replies only when a more direct answer might tend to reflect upon the manner in which the railroad is conducted.

In answer to the question of the coroner, Mr. Hobbs told of his first intimation of the wreck. He was at supper in the Hotel Joyce, in Baltimore, he said, when notified over the telephone that the disaster had occurred. His first action was to go to the train dispatcher's office at the Camden Station, where he found T. F. Dent in charge.

Hobbs Hurried to Scene

"On my arrival," continued Mr. Hobbs, "I was informed that extra East engine 2120, with a train of empty equipment, had struck No. 66 at Terra Cotta. Mr. Dent had already ordered a relief train and doctors to proceed from Washington to the scene of the wreck. I then took the first train I could get from Baltimore and went to the wreck."

"What investigation into the cause and responsibility for the accident have you made in your official capacity?" inquired Coroner Nevitt.

"None," replied Mr. Hobbs.

"Why not?" asked the coroner.

"Because," Mr. Hobbs rejoined, "upon my arrival at Takoma I found that the train crew of 2120 had been arrested and removed."

Being still further pressed as to the reason why the railroad company had not as yet instituted an investigation, Mr. Hobbs stated that as soon as the coroner's inquest is finished, the company will make a thorough investigation, but that at this time, nothing has been done.

"Were you not aware," asked the coroner, " that the crew was under arrest at the Tenth precinct police station, where they were accessible to you if you wanted to interview them?"

"Yes," was a more or less evasive reply, " but I could not make a thorough investigation under the circumstances."

Hobbs Interviewed Conductor

Through further questions, it was brought out that Supt. Hobbs had interviewed Conductor Hoffmeier of the extra when at the scene of the accident.

"I did not see Conductor Hoffmeier," admitted Mr. Hobbs. "He was in custody and was just being taken away from the scene of the wreck by the police. I asked him what kind of signals he saw at Takoma, and he replied that none were visible on account of the fog."

Mr. Hobbs was then questioned in regard to the rule of the company touching upon cases like that presented at Takoma. He produced a rule showing that when an engineer sees no signal lights at the station or tower where such lights were expected or should have been displayed he should stop the train and investigate.

The coroner then questioned the witness upon the conditions governing operator Phillips' time of duty at Takoma. It was brought out that Phillips is supposed to be on duty from 6:30 in the morning until 6:30 at night. In explaining the reasons for the adoption of this "day-operator" system, Mr. Hobbs said it was to facilitate the movement of trains during the hours when traffic is most congested.

Takoma Block Only Open Days

"Then the Takoma block is not in use after 6:30?" queried Coroner Nevitt.

"No, sir," was the emphatic reply.

Further questions divulged the facts regarding the closing of University block at 7 o'clock and the working of the Silver Spring-Rhode Island avenue section as one block during the rest of the night hours.

"These blocks, then are temporarily eliminated?" was asked.

Mr. Hobbs replied affirmatively. He was then asked as to the hours of the operator at Takoma and said that Phillips was supposed to be on duty twelve hours. The block at Silver Spring, operating the full twenty-four hours, said Mr. Hobbs, was in charge of three operators, each working an eight-hour shift. This was done to comply with the laws of Maryland, said the superintendent, which compel the railroads to work their employees only eight hours a day.

"What signal does an operator of a day block leave when he goes home?" was the next question.

"None at all," replied Mr. Hobbs. "He puts all his station lights out and drops his semaphores."

Then followed a mass of questions on technicalities that led up to the question as to what Engineer Hildebrand should expect in the way of signals at Takoma.

"If the engineer of 2120 received a white light at Silver Springs at 6:28, and when he arrived at Takoma he saw no signal at all, what would he be supposed to understand by that?" was asked at the instigation of Assistant District Attorney Turner.

Might Assume Block Clear

"If the Takoma station appeared to be closed and the lights out, he might assume he had a clear block to the University," was Mr. Hobbs' admission.

"To what do you ascribe the cause of the accident?" was the gist of an all-important question suddenly shot at Mr. Hobbs.

The superintendent could not be tricked into a hasty reply, and after deliberating for over a minute, he ventured the opinion that he would ascribe it to a 'violation of the rules.'"

"What rules?" came next.

"I am unable to say, because there has, as yet, been no thorough investigation," was the smooth rejoinder.

In answer to a final question Mr. Hobbs intimated that on Sunday night, the block at Silver Springs was in charge of a substitute operator, but that the other stations concerned were in charge of the regular men.

After a report by Preston C. Dey, of the Weather Bureau, showing "light to dense fogs" to have prevailed Sunday night, the coroner ordered a recess.

Galloway Takes Stand

The first witness to be put on the stand at the afternoon session was General Superintendent of Transportation Galloway. He was first questioned at to the difference between the manual block system as in use on the Metropolitan branch and the automated system installed on the Philadelphia division of the Baltimore and Ohio Railroad. Mr. Galloway explained that the manual system, operated by hand, was a positive system and that the automatic was a "permissive" system. This, he said, means that the manual stop signal is a positive stop, while the red of an automatic block merely holds the engineer one minute, after which he is to proceed cautiously until some other signal is shown.

He was then questioned as to when he first heard of the wreck, and stated that he was eating dinner at his home in Relay, Md., when at about 7:35 he received a telephone call telling him of the disaster.

'Would fog affect the color of a red signal light, making it appear white or greenish?" abruptly asked the coroner.

"No, sir," replied Mr. Galloway.

"Is there any order to engineers and trainmen in general to use extra cause during fogs?" was then asked.

Mr. Galloway admitted that there was no general order but that trainmen were taught to "exercise care at all times."

Must Not Pass Red Signals

"Has an engineer any right to pass a red signal or any signal without clearly understanding its significance?" asked the coroner.

"No," was the reply.

"What is done by the company if such a case occurs?" queried the coroner.

"It is such a rare occurrence that my experience is limited in this respect, and I can hardly answer that question," replied Mr. Galloway.

The coroner then showed Mr. Galloway Phillips' block sheet on which was noted that engine 2120 "went by red target."

"What would you do in case you received a report as this?" asked the coroner.

"I would take the train crew out of service and investigate the matter," was the firm reply.

Mr. Galloway said he had never received such a report in his experience.

"Is there any penalty for being behind time?" was then asked.

"No," was the rejoinder.

During the hearing of Mr. Hobbs, the coroner had asked many questions concerning the delay of the railroad officials in sending out the morgue train for the dead. He had intimated that if there was it was due to the alleged fact that the railroad officials were waiting for the coroner's permission to remove the bodies.

Need Not Wait for Coroner

This had prompted the coroner to repeat his statement already published to the effect that such excuses were absurd, inasmuch as he, the coroner, had never enforced the law in cases of accidents. Coroner Nevitt also stated that he had learned on the night of the wreck that the railroad company had arranged to have the undertakers of the city send their wagons out to remove the dead instead of sending out a second train.

This arrangement, the coroner said, he had stopped because he wanted the bodies to be brought to the morgue, where they would be centralized for identification.

The coroner then referred to the morgue train in questioning Mr. Galloway. The superintendent skillfully avoided answering the questions in such way as to reflect upon the manner in which the removal of the dead was conducted by the railroad officials, and the coroner finally dropped that tack.

The matter of block signals was reopened, and Mr. Galloway was asked to explain the meaning of the various signals at night. The use of torpedoes, fuses, and other emergency signals were referred to and explained by Mr. Galloway.

"When are they used?" asked the coroner.

"When a train is for some reason not running on schedule –through breakdowns and other unavoidable delays," was the reply.

"What should an engineer of an extra do from station to station?" next asked Coroner Nevitt.

"If he has orders to run as an extra, he should use his judgment as to speed, always, of course, to act in accordance with the block signals," replied the railroad official.

"Do you know whether the engineer of 2120 had any knowledge or should have had any knowledge that 66 was running ahead of him?"

Knew 66 Was Ahead of Him

"I believe so. He was at Washington Junction when 66 left. He stayed there until 66 cleared the block at Tuscarora, and then he had to remain still longer, as No. 1, the Cincinnati and St. Louis Limited, going West, had not cleared the block, and as it was a single track, 2120 could not proceed until No. 1 reached Washington Junction."

Then followed questions and answers regarding what happened when 66 met No. 1, none of which had any direct bearing on the accident at Terra Cotta.

"What is the duty of train dispatchers in the way of informing extra trains of other trains ahead of them?" was the next important question.

"Extra trains watch the official time card and receive no special orders, as a rule," replied Mr. Galloway.

"How, then, would the extra train crew know that the train in front was late and drawing nearer all the time?" queried the coroner.

"In this specific case, the engineer of 2120 might have known that No. 66 was late on Sunday, as No. 66 always runs behind the schedule on account of stopping at every station," said Mr. Galloway.

"How long has Hildebrand been employed by the Baltimore and Ohio Railroad?" was asked.

"Approximately twenty-three years," was replied.

It was then brought out that Hildebrand has had twelve years' experience on the Metropolitan branch the last two years as a passenger engineer.

Considered Hildebrand a Good Man

"We have always regarded him as one of the most competent men on the road," continued Mr. Galloway, in response to a question concerning Hildebrand's reputation.

"Do you know of any law regulating speed in the District of Columbia?" asked Coroner Nevitt.

"I know of a city regulation setting a limit of ten miles an hour," replied Mr. Galloway, somewhat evasively.

Mr. Galloway was then questioned as to the percent of grade from Silver Spring to Takoma, which, he said, was, approximately, forty feet to the mile, and that from Takoma to Terra Cota, which he placed at about the same degree. In response to further questioning, he said that he though the grade from Barnesville to Tuscarora was steeper.

The coroner then returned to the subject of torpedoes and fuses, and asked if the crew of 66 should not have used them when at Terra Cotta.

"No," replied Mr. Galloway, " they were running on schedule. The fact that 66 was late does not mean it was not on schedule."

"Should not 66 have known of the proximity of 2120?' asked the coroner.

"That is a question I can't answer," was the reply.

Describes Duties of Extra Crews

Mr. Galloway was then asked to describe the duties of a train crew. From his statements, it was to be inferred that the engineer and the conductor are equally responsible for the observation of signals under ordinary circumstances but that there are times when the engineer is chiefly responsible. It was inferred that on Sunday night Engineer Hildebrand was more responsible for signals than Conductor Hoffmeier. This inference was shattered when, at the instigation of Assistant District Attorney Turner; Mr. Galloway was asked directly:

"Was it the duty of Conductor Hoffmeier, of 2120 to see the signal at Takoma?"

"Yes," declared the witness.

Then several questions were asked Mr. Galloway tending to show whether or not Hildebrand should have been expecting a signal at Takoma. Mr. Galloway's testimony was hardly clear on this point. At first he said that Hildebrand, having received the signal at Sliver Spring that the block was clear to Takoma, it then being 6:28 pm, should have expected further signals at Takoma. When was pointed out that he did not reach Takoma until after the usual closing time of the block. Mr. Galloway said that Hildebrand should have looked for a signal anyway as it is a general rule that engineers should always watch for signals. If there is any rule through which Hildebrand might have been certain that under those circumstances Phillips would be at his post and signals were to be expected. Mr. Galloway did not show it clearly.

Road's Surgeon Reports

Dr. L. L. Battle, the surgeon of the Baltimore and Ohio Railroad, was then called and read a report on the relief work for the injured, of which he had charge, Sunday night.

Train Dispatcher Dent was then called and produced the telegraphic train record on which the movement of every train on the Metropolitan branch on the day of the accident is recorded. He was asked to read the report of the progress of 2120 from Washington Junction to Terra Cotta. The report showed that 2120 left Washington Junction at 5:27, Tuscarora at 5:35, Dickerson at 5:41, Barnesville at 5:46, Boyds at 5:52, Germantown at 5:58, Gaithersburg at 6:07, Rockville at 6:16, Kensington at 6:23, Silver Springs at 6:28 and Takoma at 6:31.

KEN ROSSIGNOL

From the figures on the train chart, it was calculated by the inquisitors that Hildebrand's average speed from Washington Junction to Silver Springs was about thirty-five miles an hour, and from Silver Springs to Terra Cotta about twenty-five miles an hour, as the engineer has maintained since the catastrophe.

"Were any specific instructions given to 2120 at Washington Junction?" was asked.

"No specific instructions, merely running orders. This train was run as an extra having no schedule to maintain or connection to make."

By further questioning, it was brought out that the only instructions given beyond the running orders referred to a freight train which 2120 caught up with and passed at Tuscarora. There were no orders regarding 66.

"Would not a double track from Germantown to Washington Junction have facilitated matters in handling the trains on Sunday?" asked Coroner Nevitt.

After mature deliberation, Mr. Dent intimated that it would have been somewhat easier to handle the traffic.

Train Record Again Referred To

The train record was again referred to, and the gradual closing up of 2120 on 66 made plain by referring to the comparative times at each station. At Washington Junction, 2120 left forty minutes behind 66; at Tuscarora, it was 42 minutes behind; at Dickerson, 30; at Barnesville, 30, at Boyds, 26; at Germantown, 25; at Gaithersburg, 22; at Rockville, 16; at Kensington, 11; at Silver Spring, 7 and at Takoma 5 minutes.

"Whose duty was it to moderate speed in this case?" was asked.

"So far as I can see, there was no necessity for 2120 slowing down. There was no danger, so long as the block signals were used and observed," replied the dispatcher.

"What signal did 66 receive at Silver Spring?" asked Coroner Nevitt.

"I can't tell; there is no record that we see to tell that," was the rejoinder.

Mr. Dent then described receiving a message direct from Phillip's at about 6:39 or 6:40 saying that 2120 had passed his red target. Mr. Dent immediately wired to University and learned that 66 had not come into that station. Knowing that something was wrong, and fearing the worst, Mr. Dent says he sat and waited until about eight minutes later, when he received word of the wreck from the conductor of 66, who had walked to University to send the dispatch. Then Mr. Dent ordered the relief train.

Through Assistant District Attorney Turner, Mr. Dent was then further questioned as to the cautionary orders, if any, that 2120 was running under, which elicited the information that 2120 had no cautionary orders of any kind.

The inquest then adjourned.

Have Confidence in Block System

The testimony of the three railroad men is looked upon as showing that the railroad authorities place implicit confidence in the block system as it is present conducted, and that no extra precautions are deemed necessary in such circumstances as existed Sunday night. The officials conducting the inquiry, while they would not commit themselves, yesterday intimated that the policy of the railroad in relying absolutely on a system that has been shown by Sunday's horror to be weak in certain respects does not appeal to them as particularly strong evidence of the railroad's lack of responsibility for the Terra Cotta tragedy.

Many highly important features are expected to be brought out today. It is believed that either Hildebrand or Phillips will be put on the stand during the day, and the railroad officials may be called for further testimony on certain points. It seems probable that the inquest will last several days.

BURY WRECK VICTIMS
Four Double and Nine Single Funerals Held
MOTHER AND SON IN CASKET

Husband and Wife Also Laid Away in Same Grave – Seventeen People Interred Here, and in Addition Services Were Held Over Wreck Victims in Other Sections

The Washington Herald

Washington, D.C. Jan. 3, 1907 - Four double and nine single funerals, all of the victims of the Sunday night catastrophe at Terra Cotta station, were held in Washington yesterday.

One of the double funerals was of a mother and her baby boy. Both were buried in the same casket, with the thirteen-month old child clasped in the mother's arms. Another was of husband and wife, both interred in a single coffin.

Two small white caskets contained the bodies of a brother and sister. The fourth double services were over a woman and her seven-year-old nephew.

The single funerals were held in all parts of the city and suburbs. In addition to the seventeen people who were buried here yesterday, funeral services were over the remains of other victims of the same disaster were held in various sections of the country.

Florists are Taxed

Coming as it did during the holidays and being followed by the forty-three deaths, the florists of Washington and the adjoining cities were taxed to their utmost to supply the demand for flowers and designs ordered by people who wished to pay their farewell tribute to the dead.

At every home, every church and every chapel where funeral services of the Terra Cotta dead were held, the floral offerings have been so numerous as to attract unusual attention.

Without the knowledge of the parent, who themselves are in hospitals, as the result of the wreck, and who are not aware of the fact that two of their little children are dead, the bodies of Annie and Frank Kunlo were laid to rest. Services were held in the morning at the chapel of Frank Geier's Sons, 1117 Seventh Street. Father S. A. B. Wunnenberg, of St. Mary's Catholic Church, officiated. The two little white caskets were placed in a temporary vault at St. Mary's Cemetery.

Residence is Deserted

Relatives, friends of the family, and schoolmates of the children attended the services yesterday morning in large numbers. The residence of the Kunlos at 18 P

Street has been deserted. Since the family went away on the eventful day, no one, with the exception of a relative or two, has had the courage to visit the residence of the family, all of whom were either injured or killed in the wreck.

On the floor of the parlor of the Kunlo home, Christmas toys, left just as the children finished playing with them, are scattered about. The little tin soldiers await the hands of a boy who will never handle them again. On a shelf lies a tiny deserted doll, once the property of Annie Kunlo, which had been put away in a pastebox by the girl herself. It has not been touched since. The pastebox is white and cold, like a little white coffin containing the remains of the dead baby – owner of the doll.

Little Joseph Kunlo was removed from Freedmen's Hospital yesterday to the Providence, where Mrs. Kunlo is confined with serious injuries. It was the first meeting since the accident. The father, John Kunlo, is at the Casualty Hospital, with both legs fractured, and his body otherwise injured. The last the parents saw of the two children was just as the terrible wreck occurred. They will never see them again. The funeral of the two children yesterday was one of the most pathetic ever held in Washington.

***

The incidents of signal blocks connected to wrecks were not isolated that year. In response to the wreck of the Terra Cotta and others, the Interstate Commerce Commission banned the use of wooden passenger coaches. The four trainmen of the two B & O trains that were in the horror at Terra Cotta were charged but later found not guilty of manslaughter.

On board the *George Washington* on the way to Norfolk the news reader provided more on news around the Chesapeake region and across the country, taking special care to report on other train wrecks.

***

"Now friends, fellow travelers and relaxing crewmembers, lend me an ear!" announced Jack Douglas.

"I have this news item now for you from Topeka Kansas, via the *Washington Herald* and dated today, Jan. 3, 1907...the weather is bitter outside, and we will still be able to make it to Norfolk as the ice cover receded from the channel today...now the news:

FORTY DIE IN WRECK

Twenty-five Hurt in Railroad Collision in Kansas
SIGNAL OPERATOR BLAMED
Forecasts the Impending Disaster and Then Flees, but Is Later Arrested –Victims were Nearly All Mexican Laborers –Cars Catch Fire and Passengers Burn to Death

TOPEKA, Kansas. Jan. 2 – About Forty passengers, mostly Mexicans, were killed, and twenty-five seriously injured in a head-on collision at 4:30 o'clock this morning, three miles west of Alma, between passengers trains No. 29, southbound, and No. 30, northbound on the Chicago, Rock Island and Pacific Railroad.

The wrecked trains were running between El Paso and Chicago.

Most of the killed and injured were on the southbound train.

The cars went into a ditch, and several of them caught fire.

Bodies Consumed in Fire

The flames consumed many of the bodies of the victims.

The injured were brought to Topeka on a relief train.

Most of the dead were Mexican laborers, who were in the smoking car on No. 29. They were en route to El Paso.

The baggage car telescoped the smoker and crashed down through the roof of the latter car, crushing out the lives of the occupants; the majority of whom were curled up in the seats and asleep.

Train No. 29 bore the brunt of the collision. The cars on No. 30 were not seriously damaged, and they were made up into a train and sent south in place of the destroyed No. 29.

Signal Operator Blamed

Blame for the collision seems to rest on John Lynes, nineteen years old, the telegraph operator at Volland. Orders had been issued for No. 29 and No. 30 to pass at Volland. These orders had been sent to the operator at Volland, who was instructed to hold No. 29 at that point. For some reason, he failed to deliver the order to No. 29, and the latter train went by, meeting No. 30 within a few miles of Volland.

Lynes had fled before the wreck occurred, after first forecasting the impending collision. Five minutes before the trains met, he wired the dispatcher as follows:

"No. 29 has gone, and I have gone also."

Then he left his key.

Even with this dispatch in hand there was no possible way of preventing the wreck.

Lynes was captured and taken to the jail at Topeka.

Both Heavy Trains

Both trains were heavy ones, having ten cars each, including Pullman sleepers and tourists, chair cars and coaches, smokers and baggage cars. No. 29 is known as the "California Fast Mail." It left Chicago at 8:30 o'clock on Tuesday morning. No. 30 is the opposite train and is known as the "Chicago Fast Mail." It left El Paso on Monday night and was due in Chicago tonight.

No. 29 was crowded to the doors with passengers, but the number of travelers on No. 30 was not large.

Relief trains and all possible succor was rushed to the scene from every available point.

Train Crew Escapes

Just before the collision Engineer McMahon and Fireman Brown, of No. 30, and Engineer Slater and Fireman Sweeney, of No. 29, jumped. All four escaped injury.

An interpreter for the Mexicans was questioned as he lay slowly burning to death under the wreckage. He said there were twenty-five Mexicans in their party going from Kansas City to El Paso to work. The most of these were burning to death. Soon after giving this information, the interpreter himself succumbed.

HILL FEARS TRAIN SYSTEM

Declares Block Rules Are Violated Constantly on All Lines

Believes Every Railroad Journey He Takes May Be His Last – "There's Danger in It," He Says

Information has been received in Washington through official channels that practically every railroad in the United States at the present time is disregarding the rules governing the operation and management of the block-signal system. Chairman Knapp said yesterday that while he had no direct information on the subject he believed that it was true that the block-signal system through design had become absolutely ineffective.

A high official of the administration, in fact, a member of the Cabinet, told this story:

"I was in New York a few weeks ago and met while there James J. Hill, a well-known railroad man. He deplored the conditions resulting in so many disasters, and rather mournfully spoke as follows:

"Every time I undertake a railroad journey nowadays I wonder whether it is to be my last. The thing has grown to be uncertain. It is a fact, of knowledge to every railroad man, that in this day from two to three trains enter at times into every block of every system in the country. There is a danger in it."

***

"There is good news in from Washington in that there are now, but 43 believed to have perished in the wreck at Terra Cotta," said Jack Douglas. "Perhaps you didn't know that Washington, D.C. has a fellow with the title of 'Morguemaster'."

CUTS DEATH LIST TO 43

Morguemaster Decides that Fragments Are Portions of Bodies

Morguemaster Schoneberger made the discovery yesterday that the supposed mangled remains of an unidentified victim of the wreck were the composite fragments of several persons. In view of the fact that no person is reported missing, it is believed that the fragments belonged to bodies that have been identified. This discovery reduces the number of victims to forty-three, all of whom are known.

Crowds of curious people went to the scene of the wreck yesterday, and so great was the throng on the tracks that the police had difficulty in preventing accidents from passing trains.

"I have yet another item involving travel by railroad, that of a train robbery which took place in the nearby Commonwealth of Virginia on a Chesapeake and Ohio train this past Sunday morning," announced Jack Douglas.

PULLMAN BANDIT CAPTURED
Man Arrested Near Richmond as He Was Returning North

SPECIAL TO THE WASHINGTON HERALD

RICHMOND, VA. Jan. 2 – A man suspected of the crime of holding up the Chesapeake and Ohio train Sunday morning and robbing the passengers in the Pullman sleeper, was arrested near here today. The man had evidently been South after committing a robbery, and was returning with Baltimore or Washington as his destination. A number of checks and papers were found on his person. The man will say nothing regarding his own personality or movements. From what can be learned, it appears that the statement that the man had an accomplice on the train is a mistake. It is believed that after shooting Conductor Abernathy and escaping from the train with his booty, the desperado boarded a train for the South, in which section he remained until he thought it safe to return.

"Now folks, if you think there are many odd personages populating the General Assemblies of

KEN ROSSIGNOL
Maryland and Virginia, I bring you this tidbit of the news from the great state of Kansas," said Jack with a chuckle.

MUST PUBLISH ENGAGEMENTS
Kansas Legislator Believes Such Law Might Prevent Divorce

Topeka, Kansas – Jan. 2. Senator Smith will introduce a bill in the legislature providing that all marriage engagements must be published in local papers and churches at least thirty days before the wedding ceremony is to be performed.

Mr. Smith presents argument to prove such a law would tend to prevent divorces, unhappy marriages, and declares it is highly satisfactory law in several European countries.

"We may find out how pugilistic our President may be if and when he accepts a proposal to be a judge of babies at the upcoming Jamestown Exposition," rattled off Jack to laughter from the audience in the grand saloon of the George Washington as it passed Coles Point, Virginia.

ROOSEVELT MAY JUDGE BABIES
Jamestown Exposition Officials Plan Unique Attraction

SPECIAL TO THE WASHINGTON HERALD

Norfolk, Va. Jan. 2 – An international baby show with President Roosevelt as chief judge and presenter of prizes will be a feature of the Jamestown Exposition, should the President accept the honor which it is proposed to bestow upon him.

Plans for the show are now being worked out by the exposition officials. It is proposed to have babies from all countries and conditions on life in the

228

competition, and there will be prizes for the fattest babies, for the prettiest babies, for the slimmest, best developed, and best formed babies. Mothers of prize babies are deeply interested in the proposition.

Epilogue

Ethan Aaron Douglas, who at the age of ten, joined his grandfather living the carefree life on a steamboat on the Chesapeake Bay. As Captain of the Savannah, Captain Douglas taught his grandson the lessons of living in harmony with weather, the Bay and the people they all met.

By 1880, Ethan was now forty years of age, had a growing family with his bride Molly they raised ten children – about the right size family for the times. Now grandchildren were soon to be appearing in this story of challenges, storms and survival as nature and calamities brightened and darkened their lives.

With much of the family working in the newspaper business and working the water on various vessels, keeping up with the news was a challenge. But not when the news readers were at work on the Old Bay Line steamships plying the waters of the Chesapeake and Potomac.

More change in America and the Chesapeake region lie ahead for both the nation and the Douglas family in CHESPEAKE 1910, arriving soon in your favorite bookstore in eBook, paperback and Audible formats.

CHESAPEAKE 1880

Main saloon of a Norfolk and Washington steamship.

Old Dominion Line at Hampton, Va. in 1905.

T

his photo of a Norfolk & Western steamship by Theodor Horydczak. Library of Congress.

The Dauntless. Frederick Coffay, Library of Congress

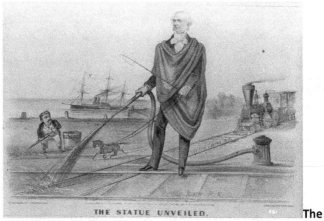

THE STATUE UNVEILED.

The "statue" is railroad giant Cornelius Vanderbilt, who in 1869 tried unsuccessfully to assume control of James Fisk's Erie Railroad by buying out its stock. Here he stands, like the Colossus of Rhodes, at the crossroads of the New York Central and the Hudson River Railroads both of which he owned. He sprays the tracks with a hose marked "270" which is attached to a hydrant. He also holds a whip and the reins of a horse. A steamship in the background symbolizes his commercial shipping interests. At left a diminutive Fisk waters his own line, the Erie, using a bucket and hand-powered pump while eyeing his competitor enviously. Library of Congress. Published by Currier & Ives, 1869.

Print showing, around the outer rim of a horseshoe, immigrants from many nations arriving by steamship, a man with a mule pulling a canal boat, two bandits on horseback robbing travelers, and within the horseshoe, a locomotive arriving on snow-covered tracks, tossing snow onto the clothing of waiting passengers. At the bottom of the print are two vignettes, identified on the color print as, on the left, "interior of world famous dining car" and on the right, "interior reclining chair car." Text on the horseshoe "Speed Comfort & Safety" is largely obscured by the coloring. Horseshoe may suggest good luck! "To all who travel by train or ship." J.M.W. Jones S. & P. Co.

COLLINS AND CUNARD.

RAISING THE WIND; OR, BOTH SIDES OF THE STORY.

Caricature of steamship line competitors Edward Knight Collins (backed by Uncle Sam) and Sir Samuel Cunard (backed by John Bull) trying to blow toy ships across the tub in opposite directions. Lithograph by Frank Bellew in the Lantern, N. Y. 1852

Print showing well-dressed passengers waiting as the Illinois Central Railroad train pulls into the station; also shows a steamship, horse-drawn carriage, stagecoach, and canal boat, along with a large globe displaying the United States and the extent of the I.C.R.R. lines. The world's railroad scene / Swain & Lewis 1882 Chicago. Illustration shows Mark Hanna wearing a sign "Please help the poor" and J.P. Morgan at the end of a pier with the "Ship Yard"

ONE YEAR AFTER

behind them, holding out their hats, one labeled "For a shipping subsidy," to Uncle Sam standing in front of the U.S. Treasury. An enormous ocean-going steamship, flying a banner " American built ships," floats offshore in the distance. By Louis Dalrymple, Puck Magazine 1901.

Illustration shows an old and haggard "Justice" sitting in a chair on a rock in the East River, cobwebs have grown over her sword, scales, and an "Indictment"; in the background, the steamship General Slocum is engulfed in flames (it burned on June 15th 1904 with a loss of over 1,000 lives).

1906 wreck of Pennsylvania Railroad train caused by malfunctioning drawbridge at Atlantic City, New Jersey.

About the Author:

Writing about true crime, a series of cruise thrillers, maritime history, and historical fiction keeps Rossignol busy. All books are in eBook, paperback and Audible editions at major retailers.

As a maritime history speaker, Rossignol enjoys meeting audiences around the world and discussing the original news stories of the sinking of the RMS Titanic and other maritime history topics.

Rossignol has appears on ships meeting folks around the world and sharing the stories of the heroes of the Titanic, the explorations of the new world voyagers, the Bermuda Triangle and the history of piracy, among other maritime history topics, which are his passion.

Rossignol appears at the Titanic Museum Attractions in Pigeon Forge, Tennessee, and Branson, Missouri for book signings and to talk with visitors about the RMS Titanic.

He has appeared on Good Morning America, ABC 20/20; ABC World News Tonight and in a 2012 production of Discovery Channel Investigation Motives & Murders Series, A Body in the Bay.

News coverage of Rossignol's landmark civil rights case, represented by Levine Sullivan Koch & Schulz re: United States Fourth Circuit Court of Appeals Rossignol v Voorhaar, 2003, included articles in most major news outlets, as well as a column by syndicated columnists James J. Kilpatrick.

A strong highway safety advocate, Rossignol also publishes the DWIHitParade.com that focuses on impaired driving and also publishes the monthly print and online regional publication, The Chesapeake Today, which is available on newsstands in Delaware, Maryland and Virginia.

News coverage of Rossignol's DWIHitParade.com won an Emmy in 2012 for WJLA reporter Jay Korff and coverage of the St. Mary's Today newspaper by WUSA reporter Bruce Leshan was awarded an Emmy in 2000.

***

Thanks for your purchase of CHESAPEAKE 1880 and please leave a review on Amazon if you enjoyed the book.

***

"Want a chance of winning the world's most advanced e-reader or a $119 Amazon Giftcard?"

Compare: No glare in bright sunlight

Unlike reflective tablet and smartphone screens, the latest Kindle Paperwhite reads like paper—no annoying glare, even in bright sunlight.

Please join us for special offers and giveaways by emailing your name and email address to: ken.thechesapeake@gmail.com.

By joining our mailing list, you will be entered into our Great Washington's Birthday Event and a chance to win an Amazon Paperwhite Kindle.

CHESAPEAKE 1880

Just by joining our mailing list, you will receive a free gift and still be eligible for our wonderful George Washington's Birthday Giveaway of an Amazon Paperwhite!

First in this series:

CHESAPEAKE 1850

Other books:

The Chesapeake: Tales & Scales

The Chesapeake: Legends, Yarns & Barnacles

The Story of The Rag

Titanic 1912

Titanic & Lusitania: Survivor Stories

Titanic Poetry, Music & Stories

KLAN: Killing America

Fire Cruise

Coke Air: Chesapeake Crime Confidential

Pirate Trials: Dastardly Deeds & Last Words

Pirate Trials: Hung by the Neck Until Dead

Cruising the Waterfront

KEN ROSSIGNOL
Boating Chesapeake Bay

Panama 1914

Leopold & Loeb Killed Bobby Franks

The Battle of Solomon's Island

Bank of Crooks & Criminals

The Marsha & Danny Jones Thrillers:

The Privateer Clause

Return of the Sea Empress

Follow Titanic

Follow Triangle

Cruise Killer